O9-BTN-500

More Praise for *The PITA Principle*

"This isn't a self-help book; it's a 'helps everybody' book, showing why people act the way they do."

—*Mike Logan, Pfizer; pharmaceutical sales rep for 40 years; industry-wide Pharmaceutical Representative of the Year (1998)*

"Well written, an engrossing read, and an excellent contribution to the professional literature on interpersonal relations in the workplace. I strongly endorse the importance of *The PITA Principle* for professionals in career development, supervisors, and general readers who are interested in personality types."

—*Edwin L. Herr, Ed.D., Distinguished Professor Emeritus of Education (Counselor Education and Counseling Psychology) and Associate Dean Emeritus, Penn State University*

"It felt good knowing that I wasn't the only one who had bosses and coworkers with those types of behaviors!"

Lieutenant Colonel Jim White, U.S. Army

"PITA is a rich metaphor that provides people with a language they can use effectively to describe difficult work experiences. Moreover, it conveys accurate impressions of these experiences in ways that bring some levity to the situation and help defuse it productively."

—*Spencer G. Niles, Department Head and Professor, Counselor Education, Counseling Psychology, and Rehabilitation Services, Penn State University; past president, National Career Development Association; editor,* Journal of Counseling & Development

"Makes valid and compelling points about how caring, empathetic leaders can be the most successful in today's workplace."

—*Paul Sanders,* Business Lexington

"Aided by scores of recognizable examples and self-evaluation exercises, *The PITA Principle* can be a book of self-discovery regarding our emotional intelligence. It should cause employers to rethink the entire hiring and people-management processes. Following the concepts in this book can make a difference!"

—*Jeffrey W. Brown, President, Comprehensive Search*

T H E

PITA

PRINCIPLE

THE

PITA

PRINCIPLE

How to Work with
and Avoid Becoming a
PAIN IN THE ASS

Robert Orndorff, D.Ed., and Dulin Clark, Ph.D.

THE PITA PRINCIPLE

© 2009 by Robert Orndorff and Dulin Clark

Published by JIST Works, an imprint of JIST Publishing
7321 Shadeland Station, Suite 200
Indianapolis, IN 46256-3923
Phone: 800-648-JIST   Fax: 877-454-7839   E-mail: info@jist.com

Visit our Web site at **www.jist.com** for information on JIST, free job search tips, tables of contents and sample pages, and ordering instructions for our many products!

Quantity discounts are available for JIST books. Have future editions of JIST books automatically delivered to you on publication through our convenient standing order program. Please call our Sales Department at 800-648-5478 for a free catalog and more information.

Trade Product Manager: Lori Cates Hand
Copy Editor: Chuck Hutchinson
Cover Designer: Lynn Miller
Interior Designer: Aleata Halbig
Proofreader: Jeanne Clark
Indexer: Cheryl Lenser

Printed in the United States of America
13 12 11 10 09 08   9 8 7 6 5 4 3 2 1

Library of Congress Cataloging-in-Publication Data

Orndorff, Robert.
    The PITA principle : how to work with and avoid becoming a pain in the ass /
Robert Orndorff and Dulin Clark.
          p. cm.
    Includes index.
    ISBN 978-1-59357-551-9 (alk. paper)
     1. Conflict management. 2. Interpersonal relations. 3. Interpersonal conflict. I.
    Clark, Dulin, 1963- II. Title.
    HD42.O76 2008
    650.1'3—dc22

                                                            2008017932

ISBN 978-1-59357-551-9

CONTENTS

Acknowledgments

From Robert Orndorff

Everybody who has written a book appreciates the sacrifice it takes, especially as it relates to the evening and weekend time away from family. I want to thank my wife, Chris; daughters Jessie and Addie; and son, Zach, for their ongoing love, support, and inspiration. Chris, thanks for being such an outstanding sounding board for me, and for your creative talents in suggesting a couple of the Honorable-Mention PITAs. Likewise, I'm grateful to my mom, dad, brother Erik, and sister Kel for humoring me as I bored them with various PITA ideas and updates.

I also want to single out some colleagues and friends who have supported me on this project. First I want to thank Dulin Clark, a close colleague and friend and my coauthor, for bearing with my Overstuffed PITA behaviors and for adding a psychological dimension and grounding to *The PITA Principle*. It's been a privilege working alongside you. Thanks to Todd Heckman, Managing Director at Smart & Associates, and his talented new consultants for inviting us to conduct our first PITA seminar and for contributing to the creation of a few Honorable-Mention PITAs. I also want to thank Gail, Donna, Hillary, Ellery, Pat, John, Ron, Maura, and my Career Services colleagues for their support and encouragement.

From Dulin Clark

The PITA Principle could not have happened without intensive brainstorming, discussing, and conceptualizing with my coauthor Bob Orndorff. We've often shared that it's likely that the project would not have happened if either of us had made a solo attempt at it. The project came to life as the result of some lively banter and the merging of two adventurous minds that wanted to address a topic that practically all workers tackle. For his ability to provide continuous enthusiasm, optimism, and humor, I thank my coauthor Bob Orndorff. Your inspirational qualities outweigh your PITA tendencies!

Secondly, I would like to thank Susan for all her support and patience throughout this project and for her sharp psychological mind. She had a way of providing me with just the right amount of support to guide me through the rough times while also providing the brainpower for adding clarity to many of the PITA concepts.

There are also a few other people who need to be recognized for their direct and indirect contributions to the book. I'd like to acknowledge my grandmother Julia Clark, my favorite author and the inspiration for all my writing. To the career counseling staff at the Penn State University career center: You guys are the best and I have appreciated your support over the past year more than words can ever express. To Dad, Mary Ellen, Meredith, Will, Gillian, and Alexa: Thanks for all your interest throughout the project. You kept asking about the "The Book" and your curiosity kept me motivated.

From Both

We would like to thank our dear friends and colleagues from JIST Publishing for the strong support they've shown toward *The PITA Principle*. We've worked most closely with Lori Cates Hand, an exceptionally strong editor, and Natalie Ostrom, a very talented PR specialist, both of whom have been absolutely wonderful to work with on this exciting project. You never called us PITAs even though there were times when you probably thought it. We appreciate your ongoing enthusiasm for *The PITA Principle* and your dedication to making it a better book. JIST is a first-class publishing company that employs some of the nicest and most talented people in the business.

Introduction

This book speaks to the human experience of performing work in groups. Anyone who has ever had a job where he or she was required to work and interact with coworkers for a significant period of time will immediately understand and gravitate to the concepts presented in the chapters that follow.

Regardless of how your collection of coworkers came into existence, either through no choice of your own or through a reasonable degree of personal input, you will run into situations in which the personalities that emerge present you with challenges. If you were to sit back and reflect on your daily interactions with people on your staff, in your unit, on your floor, near your office, or on your project team, you would immediately be reminded of that person or persons who try your nerves and interpersonally challenge you beyond the norm. Instantly, a person's name or face pops into your head. You think about the strained interactions, the feedback you may have provided, the lack of receptivity to your feedback, how that person talks, how he or she listens (or doesn't listen), the way that person uses or misuses your valuable time, or the way you obsessively strategize about your one-on-one discussions with him or her.

Right now, you are no doubt saying something like, "Oh God, yes, do I ever know that person." And you are not alone. Rest assured that right now many other people who are reading this introduction are having the same immediate reaction as you. Someone they work with is a real pain in their ass—or PITA, for short. But short of finding a new job, they don't have the option of getting away from those people. Instead, they have to find a way to work with the PITAs.

Two Critical Career Success Factors

With educational backgrounds in counseling and psychology and close to 20 years as career development specialists, managers, trainers, and supervisors, we have come to strongly believe in two critical factors of career success: facing adversity externally with coworkers, bosses, and employees; and facing it internally with our own personality issues and functional weaknesses.

The first success factor deals with building and maintaining productive relationships with difficult coworkers. Let's face it: Anyone can build and maintain positive relationships with coworkers who are hardworking, pleasant, thoughtful, respectful, and fun to work with. It takes a true professional to establish healthy relationships with coworkers who are cynical, needy, disorganized, conceited, and self-centered.

The second critical success factor focuses on increasing your own self-awareness of areas that need improvement. Through supervising, training, and coaching thousands of college students, employees, and adults in career transition, we have found it clear that those who consistently take a hard, honest look at themselves while reflecting on their work performance and behaviors are in a much better position to make substantive improvements and enhance the quality of their performance. We have yet to meet the perfect professional, so until we do, we all must realize that everyone has areas of strength and areas that they need to constantly work on.

How This Book Is Organized

Chapter 1 provides an overview of *The PITA Principle,* including a detailed description of the two categories of PITAs featured in the book:

- **P**ains **I**n **T**he **A**ss

- **P**rofessionals **I**ncreasing **T**heir **A**wareness

Also, because self-awareness is such an important concept throughout the book, we delve into this area by providing some perspectives and research about it.

In chapters 2 through 8, you will dive into the different types of PITAs—seven in all. This is the real "meat" inside *The PITA Principle*. Each chapter describes a unique type of PITA. We chose these PITA types because we believed that they were the best examples of the PITAs in most workplaces, and so they should have universal appeal. From Crusty PITAs to Soggy PITAs to Sloppy PITAs, you'll learn plenty about each type of PITA. More importantly, you'll be exposed to coping strategies that will help you build more effective working relationships with each type of PITA coworker. Then, for each of the seven PITAs, you'll also learn about strategies to avoid becoming a PITA yourself, or at least lessen your potential for behaving like a PITA.

In chapter 9, we present a case study of a Combo PITA who incorporates characteristics from several different PITA types. The Combo PITA chapter illustrates the point that most workers have more than one PITA type associated with them. Although there's typically a primary PITA type that best describes many of your coworkers, it's important to consider the secondary PITA types in play as well when determining how to better work with them.

Chapter 10 is a sampler platter of "honorable-mention" PITAs. In this chapter, you will have fun learning about 10 other PITA types that didn't quite make it as "entrée" PITAs, but rather more like appetizer PITAs. These mini PITAs aren't full fledged PITA coworkers—they just sort of gnaw away at you over time and are somewhat annoying.

In chapters 11 and 12, through an informal PITA survey and some other practical exercises, you will explore your own challenges and difficulties in coping with specific PITA types. This will help you think about the personalities that give you the most trouble. You will also be able to determine which PITA type you might most resemble, along with the work situations and people that tend to bring out the PITA behaviors in you. Once you have explored your own PITA profile, you will be exposed to some practical methods for working on any PITA tendencies you might have and on working more effectively with the PITAs who give you the most trouble. You'll end by developing your own systematic plan of action, which will get you on your way to building healthier working relationships with your toughest PITA coworkers and minimizing your own potential to behave like a PITA in certain work situations.

CHAPTER 1

Understanding the PITA Principle

This chapter lays the groundwork for the later chapters that describe different types of difficult coworkers and how to deal with them. It begins by making the distinction between good PITAs and bad PITAs. Then it addresses why it's important to understand the PITAs in your life, as well as have a healthy self-awareness of your own PITA tendencies.

Even the coworkers who are a huge pain in your ass do have some redeeming qualities, so this chapter discusses how to identify these positives and use them to your best advantage. It's important to appreciate that everyone is different and that different isn't always bad.

Two Types of PITAs

The acronym *PITA* humorously captures the two categories of people that we want to present in the book. The first PITA category is the challenging one, the one that makes you squeeze stress balls and rub your temples. The second category of PITA is the good one, the one to which we should all aspire. The following sections describe the characteristics of the two PITA categories.

Pain In The Ass

The first category of PITA is based on those often awkward, difficult, unpleasant, frustrating, and emotionally draining interactions with specific people in your organization. In this case, the acronym PITA is understood by many to mean "PAIN IN THE ASS." We were drawn to the expression because it speaks a universal language. It says it all in a few simple words. It captures and expresses our annoyances in such a satisfying way. It is a language spoken in private office chats, in whispered exchanges in mailrooms, at happy hours, during dinner-table discussions, or through self-talk in the most private recesses of our own minds.

PAIN IN THE ASS! It speaks to the real but unfortunate truth: that days, weeks, months, and years of frustrating interactions with some coworkers puts them into a category that's easy to quantify, easy to understand, and easy to communicate to others who sympathetically understand our plight. These folks who arouse our emotions, challenge our patience, and make us labor for our money on a daily basis are simply known as PITAs.

Now, let us be clear that it is not our ultimate goal to callously tack disparaging labels on people or put people down. Rather, our goal is to provide you with some coping strategies in dealing more constructively with different types of difficult coworkers.

Professionals Increasing Their Awareness

Another goal is to strategize against becoming someone else's "pain in the ass." We do not want you to land, and most importantly stay, on another person's PITA list. We would rather you possess the self-awareness and undergo the honest self-analysis that it takes to either avoid or emerge from being a PITA. We would rather you be associated with a PITA of a different kind:

our second category of PITA, which stands for "Professionals Increasing Their Awareness." These are people who are courageous enough to look at themselves in an honest way, who realize that no one is perfect, and who are open to exploring ways to address their interpersonal and communicative deficits.

It's important to acknowledge that PITAs of the Pain In The Ass variety do exist in a variety of types and behaviors. It's equally, if not more, important to understand that the only way to avoid this colorful label is to work on being more self-aware, less defensive, and more willing to take an honest look at how well you are relating to others.

The Importance of Self-Awareness

One of the primary concepts at the foundation of *The PITA Principle* is the importance of self-awareness. The roots of psychology are firmly grounded in the notion of self-awareness as the path to ultimate growth and "choicefulness" as a thinking human being.

Freud was the first to describe and promote self-awareness (consciousness) as having the power to free a person from the forces that dominate and control individual behavior. Although his theory has been vigorously challenged on the grounds that he placed too much emphasis on sexual and aggressive drives that dictate behavior, few psychologists doubt his core theoretical assumption that unconscious material such as feelings, behaviors, and memories need to be explored and made conscious before real psychological progress can occur. Today, therapeutic professionals essentially view heightened self-understanding as synonymous with psychological maturity.

It's understood that most of us who encounter and cope with problematic workplace behaviors don't have professional backgrounds and training in the psychology of personality. However, it's not hard to buy into good common sense, and common sense dictates that we can come to understand and change only those behaviors that we accept and know to be true. Whether we're speaking about our own behaviors or the behaviors of our coworkers, it is essential that we develop the capacity to see ourselves and others honestly and to be courageous enough to acknowledge our own areas of ineffectiveness and struggle.

Although easily stated, this process seems to pose one of the greatest challenges to humankind. Heightened self-awareness, or lack of, appears to mystify some of society's most prominent figures, from the corporate executive who unknowingly yet chronically berates his employees through abuses of power, to the physician who patronizes her patients through her intellectual arrogance, to the politician who cannot and will not admit mistakes in judgment out of ego-preserving stubbornness.

M. Scott Peck, the renowned author of *The Road Less Traveled* (1978) and *A World Waiting to Be Born* (1994), astutely recognized that interpersonal difficulties and personality clashes between coworkers are highly complex and deeply disruptive features of organizations; they require skilled interventions that ideally lead to heightened awareness and increased organizational functioning. Peck, a highly respected psychiatrist, understood that increasing self-awareness was a necessary condition for any long-term behavioral change to stick. Whether we are talking about our work unit; our civic group; our church; or our city, state, or federal government, everyone needs to bring an elevated degree of "mindfulness" to his or her own work behaviors in order for organizations to function properly.

Emotional Intelligence Research and Self-Awareness

Daniel Goleman's book *Working with Emotional Intelligence* (1998) was the first to attempt to capture a broad and rather difficult-to-define set of characteristics that describe a person's interpersonal and psychological effectiveness in the workplace. Goleman has claimed that 67 percent of effective performance in the workplace can be attributed to the concept of emotional intelligence (EI), whereas 90 percent of effectiveness in leadership jobs can be accounted for by EI. At the core of emotional intelligence as defined by Goleman is this very concept of self-awareness. In the end, we view self-awareness as a person's ability to know and understand his or her own thoughts, feelings, and behaviors while also understanding how he or she impacts other people.

The concept of self-awareness is measured in different ways in the EI literature. One popular method is to complete a scale or rating about your personal qualities and then compare those results to the way you are rated on the same scales by a group of coworkers. People with high or accurate self-awareness would come closer to the ratings that a reliable set of coworkers would give them.

In a compelling study by Shipper, Kincaid, Rotondo, and Hoffman (2003) in the *International Journal of Organizational Analysis,* the authors set out to determine whether self-awareness was related to managerial effectiveness in three separate cultures: the United States, the United Kingdom, and Malaysia. The study measured self-awareness by the degree to which manager ratings agreed with subordinate ratings on their ability to interact well (for example, communicate, coach, and support) with employees. The results of the study revealed that when there was greater agreement between managers and subordinates on how well they interacted in the workplace, the managers were rated higher in terms of managerial effectiveness. Interestingly, even if managers and subordinates agreed that the managers' interactive skills were poor, they were seen as better managers than if there were disagreement among the ratings. The explanation is that when managers were aware that their interactive skills were low, they worked to overcome their deficiencies or to compensate in some other ways.

Another study by Shipper and Dillard (2000) in the *Human Resource Management Journal* appears to corroborate the Shipper *et al.* (2003) study in that high-performing managers are seemingly more self-aware. More so than lower-performing managers, they are more accurately able to estimate their own skill levels based on results from 360-degree feedback in their organizations.

But It Might Take More Than Self-Awareness Alone

Motivating a person not to engage in PITA behavior takes more than just being self-aware. To some degree, people have to be aware of themselves, their internal states, and their effect on other people in their organization, and actually care about their impact on other people. There needs to be some degree of motivation for people not only to notice and understand themselves but also to change if necessary. A study by Rode *et al.* (2007) in the *Journal of Organizational Behavior* found that "conscientiousness" or "the desire to do well" had a positive effect in the areas of group behavioral effectiveness and public speaking when combined with emotional intelligence. In essence, emotional intelligence in itself was not enough for making gains in performance. A degree of conscientious motivation was also necessary.

So this brings us to a final point. Workers need to both be self-aware about potential PITA behavior and actually *care* about not engaging in that behavior. A solid body of research that evolved out of Goleman's book on EI seems to suggest that emotional intelligence and higher degrees of self-awareness make for more effective workers. Yet we are also aware that the will or determination not to engage in particular behaviors, even if there is an awareness about the behaviors, is also necessary for positive changes to occur. We are encouraged that the literature suggests that higher degrees of self-awareness point to better-rated professionals. Better-rated professionals more frequently get rewarded by better pay increases and promotions. So this is definitely where the "rubber meets the road." People pay attention when money is at stake.

Why It's Important to Understand the PITAs in Your Life

Each PITA chapter includes a section on understanding the different PITA types. You might wonder why understanding a PITA is an important component of coping with the PITA. Why not just act or respond, you might ask. We believe that by understanding a difficult person or a specific interaction with a difficult person, you increase your likelihood of having a more desirable outcome. Often by understanding the source of a problem or by understanding some of the needs, objectives, or personality of the PITA, you can tailor your response based on a reasoned strategy instead of just reacting emotionally. In essence, coping with or confronting a difficult PITA is really a negotiation in which two parties are working toward a personally advantageous outcome.

A number of researchers and authors have addressed the importance of understanding on negotiations, influencing others, and
mediation. Ogilvie and Carsky (2002) in the *International Journal of
Conflict Management* proposed a set of exercises to help with developing greater awareness, understanding, and ability to manage
emotions while negotiating. The simulated exercises that they
propose operate on the concept that strong negative emotions,
such as anger, do not lead to the most desirable outcomes. Instead,
they often lead to retaliation. Their approach, which we also
endorse, is to attempt to understand the reasons for the other person's actions. Through having some cognitive framework for
your PITA's motivations, you have a better chance of making
proactive responses rather than heated reactive responses.

It is particularly important when dealing with a PITA who is in a
position of power, such as a supervisor or manager, that you think
through responses and approaches as opposed to merely reacting.
Again, an attempt at understanding your particular PITA can help
create a more reasoned approach—or at least a less heated or agitated approach. To this end, Yukl and Falbe (1990) in the *Journal
of Applied Psychology* concluded that understanding the goals and
objectives of the supervisor and attempting to appeal to those
goals may result in having a better chance at influencing the
supervisor in positive ways and bringing him or her in line with
your way of thinking.

However, if your PITA is more of a peer in terms of power in the
organization, a more forceful, direct approach may create a better
payoff. Regardless of how tactfully or strategically you approach
your PITA, spending some time with "developing understanding" will in the end serve you better than approaching interactions emotionally.

We are particularly drawn to the idea of developing insight into the PITA and offering an understanding of the motivations behind the different PITA styles. This information helps us understand our PITAs as well as our reactions to these PITAs.

In the end, our relationships with our particular PITAs are important to us either because their cooperation is required for us to get our work done successfully or because they have some kind of power over our jobs and careers. We might value and even like our relationships with our PITAs if their PITA behavior has not gotten too out of hand. We'd like them even better if we knew how to deal with their PITA tendencies.

Is There Anything Positive About PITA Behavior?

So, what's the big deal about being a pain in the ass? On the our face it appears that many of these types get what they want from life. For example, in many instances the pushy, abrasive, complaining, and self-absorbed personalities get people to act and react on their behalf to secure the many things that they want. After all, the number of PITAs who occupy the ranks of the rich, the powerful, and the famous are certainly no fewer than in any other walks of life.

We agree that certain characteristics such as assertiveness, determination, competitiveness, and risk-taking are highly correlated with organizational and financial success. The brazen, have-no-fear go-getter seems to be a pretty common figure in the highly competitive American free-enterprise system. Certainly, there are those who hold the opinion that "asshole" behavior and other equally colorful ways of acting are essential for getting ahead in a highly competitive, "dog-eat-dog" world. One would not have to look far to point out these rascals in the boardrooms of business, the high offices of government, or on the professional athletic fields.

Yet, there seems to be something fundamentally wrong with the notion of achievement at all costs. At some point, the unexamined and unchecked personality might win many short-term battles; ultimately, however, there will be a trail of individuals and groups who feel frustrated, weakened, and diminished by their interactions with this kind of person. When these people happen to be part of the same organization or team, major adverse effects are likely in the long run—both in terms of morale and general effectiveness.

Useful features associated with each of the particular PITA styles are presented in the following chapters. Even the more abrasive, more needy, more disorganized, or more entitled styles can bring a dose of something positive to the organization. The goal, though, is to increase the size of that dose by curbing some of the more destructive tendencies and making these people more aware of their organizational impact.

Appreciation of Differences

One of the most remarkable and fascinating aspects about people at work and work behaviors in general is that it takes a variety of personalities to make an organization run well. Noted vocational psychologists such as John Holland, Isabel Briggs Myers, and Katherine Cook Briggs spent the bulk of their careers identifying and measuring the interests, behavioral patterns, and unique qualities in people who choose different occupational areas and take on different work roles.

Generally speaking, they were affirming of all the types of personalities that make up the different occupational areas. They recognized that people who become plumbers, scientists, sculptors, teachers, stockbrokers, and tax accountants all have unique contributions to make to the world of work and to organizations. They also recognized that people who tended toward these different work personalities possessed characteristics that were both highly functional and potentially problematic. Holland, Myers, and Briggs were able to understand the tension of opposites; that is, they knew that for every positive attribute a person exhibited, there was an equally relevant deficit.

These researchers very much understood the yin and yang of work personalities. For example, for every biochemist or physicist who is revered for her analytical brilliance and adherence to strict methodology, there might also be a tendency for her to be overly critical, cold, or distant. Similarly, for every social worker who is loved for his empathy, kindness, and soft-heartedness, there is also the potential for him to be over-involved with his clientele or to have difficulty with analytical thinking or rational detachment. The point is that we can't have it all and we can't be everything!

So, how does this all relate to the PITA? The answer is that it all comes back to *awareness*. The scientist who is aware of her tendencies toward critical, rational, and detached thinking can, we hope, understand that there are other softer sides within her that she needs to develop—or at least value in other people. Likewise, the highly feeling-oriented social worker who is aware that he can be overly sympathetic and nurturing at times recognizes that he needs to develop the rational, objective side within himself.

PITAs who are "Pains In The Ass" don't get the importance of developing the other side of themselves because they are either

too self-absorbed, too unaware, or too defensive to let other information enter into their consciousness. Conversely, "Professionals
Increasing Their Awareness" are on the path of admitting and
acknowledging their deficits and understanding that they need to
be in a constant state of self-reflection, self-improvement, and
receptivity to feedback.

We Can All Be PITAs

It's natural that we all have the potential to really annoy a coworker now and again. For example, one of the authors would agree
that he is highly conceptual by nature and that he feels most comfortable in the world of ideas and possibilities, with a tendency
toward inward thinking and reflection. As a psychologist and
writer, he finds these qualities are necessary and valued in order to
conduct the business of studying people and their behaviors and
to describe these observations through the written word.
However, as an administrator and supervisor of a human services
unit, he realizes these qualities can get in the way of being fully
present.

On numerous occasions the author has been reminded that he is
often "in his head" and as a result is not always hearing the things
going on around him. This has left him in the embarrassing situation of asking questions about topics that were already discussed
just minutes before he asked the question. This no doubt makes
him a PITA of a minor degree to the people who feel unheard in
those situations and who have to repeat themselves to the inwardly drawn, outwardly inattentive supervisor.

So, what keeps the counseling supervisor from becoming a major
pain in the ass in the hearts and minds of the people that he super-
vises? The answer is twofold. First, the behavioral pattern of being

inwardly drawn to personal thoughts and musings and of not listening and paying attention to those around him is not pervasive enough to constitute a major problem. That is, it just doesn't happen often enough to *really* annoy people. Second, the counseling supervisor is aware enough of his interaction style and his tendency to be in his head that he tries to counter his natural tendencies by mindfully and consciously staying present during important interactions with his counseling staff.

The particular author being discussed owes a great debt of gratitude to his coworker for the corrective feedback he once provided. Without this feedback, or without his willingness to fully consider and respond to these observations, he could be more of a PITA to his counseling staff than he might have realized or desired.

All of us have an area of deficit whereby we annoy our coworkers now and again. In times of personal or organizational stress, these areas of deficit can become more pronounced and pervasive and create greater tensions with our coworkers. It is our responsibility to ourselves, to our coworkers, and to our organizations to get feedback on our areas of deficit, to consider these messages in nondefensive ways, and to work on developing ourselves without shame or resentment. This is the path of "Professionals Increasing Their Awareness." This is the fundamental mechanism of the PITA conversion.

For Those with Jobs and Those Just Starting

Thus far, the emphasis has been on current employees becoming aware of their own problematic behaviors and the behaviors of their coworkers in order to create more functional organizations. Certainly, the current workplace or past places of employment provide the most real-life examples on which to reflect and explore PITA behavior. The degree of some of these problems doesn't often reveal itself until after we have worked for a while and become seasoned professionals with many experiences to draw upon.

Yet, in many ways *The PITA Principle* is meant to be preventative and prescriptive for the younger culture of high school and college graduates who are about to enter the work force. Employers are recognizing that the softer skill sets such as effective communications, interpersonal relations, and integrity are just as important, if not more so, as the harder technical and business skills. They look for graduates who can function on teams, lead and influence people, make sound and ethical decisions, and stay composed and professional under pressure.

To this end, it is imperative that younger professionals learn to evaluate their behaviors with regard to their impact on their coworkers, their supervisors, and their supervisees, in addition to their general abilities to perform well in their respective job functions. Learning to seek out and receive feedback from a trusted colleague could be one of the most important tasks the new professional ever undertakes. Perhaps this colleague is the immediate supervisor, a mentor, or some other person who has been sought out because he or she has good judgment. No matter who the person is, checking in regularly to discuss performance is the right path to becoming more self-aware about workplace behaviors.

CHAPTER 2

The Sealed PITA:
A Closed-Off Coworker Who Doesn't Want Your Feedback

I f you've ever attempted to pry open an uncut pita-bread pocket, you understand the difficulty associated with creating a functional opening where none exists. Aside from the messy process of prying, probing, and tearing, creating a result that is ultimately worse than the original state, there appears to be little that you can do with the sealed pita. The payoff doesn't seem to be worth the effort. In the end, the pita is left alone in the crumby aftermath of the struggle, or dumped, and a better, more workable alternative is considered (like maybe a tortilla).

The sealed concept accurately describes many PITAs in the workplace. These folks have no opening available for feedback, constructive criticism, suggestions for improvement, discussions about strengths and weaknesses, or real opportunities for development. Sealed PITAs simply will not allow for it. In essence, we are talking about a lack of self-awareness and an inability or unwillingness to allow for an opening where a meaningful exchange can occur. Sealed PITAs have closed themselves off from any responsibility for making a workplace exchange better, easier, or more productive.

Ultimately, it's the lack of ownership of interpersonal responsibility that is the hallmark of the Sealed PITA. The fault almost always lies with someone else, an external situation, too much work, poor resources, a lack of understanding, or even *you*, if you dare probe the Sealed PITA too hard.

The Sealed PITA is a common thread among all other PITA types, which is why it's the first PITA in the book. Being closed off represents a fundamental obstacle for all the other PITAs as well. There must be an opening somewhere in the person for change to occur. Remember, a person doesn't become a pain in the ass by merely engaging in an undesirable behavior now and again. One becomes a PITA by repeating the same frustrating and problematic behaviors over and over again, reflecting either a lack of awareness; an unwillingness to change; or no consistent, cohesive plan for making change happen.

Addressing the sealed part, that which is closed and shut down, presents the greatest challenge. However, by opening the closed parts, we create opportunities to work on the areas that are keeping us from performing better. It also allows us to establish more workable relationships with our colleagues.

A Working Definition for the Sealed PITA

A Sealed PITA is a coworker who is closed off and defensive about receiving feedback. He or she is generally on guard (to an extreme degree) when it comes to receiving constructive criticism. Throughout this chapter we refer to people who display these characteristics as "sealed." Any situations that might tend to cause sealed behavior are called "sealed situations."

The Sealed PITA at Work

Whether you are a coworker trying to complete a team project, a supervisor working to provide better customer service, or a worker feeling disgruntled by unfair treatment, you have no doubt tangled with a Sealed PITA. To highlight the dynamics of the Sealed PITA, consider the following workplace scenario between a shift nurse and a director of nursing.

Susan was a relatively new hire at a nursing home, where she was one of three nurses who worked the 3–11 shift on weekdays. She had a reputation with her coworkers and supervisors of being average in performance based on her efficiency, accuracy, willingness to pitch in, and other informal measures. There were no problems with her overall patient care: She administered medications accurately and applied treatments effectively.

Famous Sealed PITAs

Here are some characters from popular television shows and movies who exemplify Sealed PITA characteristics:

- Bebe Neuwirth as Dr. Lilith Sternin-Crane *(Cheers)*

- Doris Roberts as Marie Barone *(Everybody Loves Raymond)*

- Sandra Oh as Dr. Cristina Yang *(Grey's Anatomy)*

- Angela Kinsey as Angela Martin *(The Office)*

Her primary deficit, however, was her low overall enthusiasm for the job and her reputation of consistently being the first one out the door at the end of the shift and the least likely to help a coworker who needed a switch in shift. Susan's reluctance to demonstrate more team-based behavior was difficult to quantify because she did adequately perform the duties required of her position.

Susan performed satisfactorily for the first few months of her employment, despite the fact that she generally appeared not to enjoy her job. Relationships with coworkers started to become strained as she solidified her reputation as someone who would not help out in a pinch. She often had excuses (for example, sore back, too tired) for not assisting with extra duties that are inherent in any job. The clincher came when she called in twice in a two-week period saying she wouldn't be in because she didn't want to drive in the snow. This behavior was problematic because it is understood in the healthcare business that staff coverage is vital and that workers should completely exhaust all possibilities before calling off work.

Susan was appropriately confronted on her behavior by the Director of Nursing (DON). The DON now had tangible behaviors to address, in addition to her colleagues' overall impression that Susan needed to be more of a team player.

"I wanted to check in with you about the two days that you called off due to snow. I know that bad weather makes it hard to get here, but as healthcare professionals we have to do our very best to get to work. We don't have quite the flexibility that other people do when it comes to bad weather. The roads were generally clear, and a couple inches is not normally cause for staying home."

Susan sat quietly with her arms folded, but was noticeably annoyed.

The DON continued. "While we're talking, I have also received some feedback from a couple people on staff that it's hard to get you to help out and go beyond the bare minimum in terms of putting in effort on the unit. I know you are aware that we work in an environment where pitching in is essential, since we are often placed in emergency situations that require multiple hands and we are usually needed on short notice. I am willing to hear you out and get your perspective. I believe you have strong clinical skills and the potential to be a good nurse, but I wanted to bring this to your attention since I've heard things from a couple of people."

At this point, it is important to note that it is not Susan's work behaviors thus far that make her a PITA, but the behaviors that follow.

Susan responded, "I cannot understand how you can treat me this way, especially since I've tried so hard over the past few months. I've worked very hard here and the patients really like me. You are not being very fair. I don't understand what you mean by pitching in and helping any more than I already do, and you know how nervous I get driving in the snow. I also think that you don't really care that I have a long drive and that my car doesn't have very good tires."

The DON replied, "I'm appreciative that you have tried hard to learn the job over the past few months and that the patients respond well to you, but there are some issues that have been raised regarding effort on the job that you need to consider. And I do care that your drive is a long one, but the critical nature of the job requires that you be here. Transportation issues are your responsibility. It's up to you to take care of those details."

Susan finished, "Well, I have never been reprimanded like this before and I can't believe that you are challenging my professionalism! You obviously are not very committed when it comes to the well-being and safety of your nursing staff."

As the conversation progressed, Susan got increasingly offended, angry, and tearful.

You can see why Susan could be viewed as a PITA of a very difficult kind. She proved to be entirely sealed off from any personal accountability. If there were any opening at all and Susan could look inward to acknowledge even part of the truth of her DON's feedback, she might not be a PITA at all. Her performance problems were certainly workable and correctable if she were willing to have an open dialogue about the issues. Instead, she was completely unwilling to consider the feedback that she was receiving.

To further complicate the issue, Susan, perhaps unconsciously, put her DON on the defensive by making her seem like the uncaring "bad guy" for even suggesting that there were problems. The degree to which Susan would become a Sealed PITA would depend on how consistent, pervasive, and problematic her Sealed posture became over time.

Ideally, the outcome of interactions such as this one leads to some sort of practical solution that has a concrete remedy. If Susan were dissatisfied with her position or her place of work, she could have considered a new position, a new challenge, or a new type of facility. Similarly, if the problem came down to a coworker issue, the DON could have figured out the source of the coworker problem, assessed it, and dealt with it. If the problem was a faulty belief about the importance of being a team player or a reliable coworker, some education about professionalism in a nursing environment, or any work environment, would have been necessary. Although these problem/solution scenarios are rarely neat and clean, there is a much greater chance of some sort of satisfactory resolution if the supervisor understands the core problem.

Understanding the Sealed PITA

No doubt the situation that the Director of Nursing encountered in this scenario is one shared by many supervisors in all industries and occupational settings. Although managing a Sealed PITA can be very difficult, it is helpful to understand the nature of the problem—more specifically, the nature of defensive reactions such as the one demonstrated in the scenario.

Sigmund Freud was the first psychologist to put a name to defensive reactions, which he referred to as *defense mechanisms*. Susan's reaction to her director's feedback was a classic defensive response to having to own any personal or professional responsibility for her behavior. The mechanism behind her defensiveness was to play on the potential guilt of her supervisor for not considering her individual life circumstances. By shifting the responsibility to her supervisor, she could regain power in the situation and take the focus off her own attitudes and behaviors.

So, you might ask why it's necessary for Susan to respond so defensively to her supervisor's seemingly harmless inquiry into her performance. This is the fundamental question that lies at the core of all defensive reactions. Although each situation is unique, the universal answer is that defense mechanisms help to ward off perceived or real threats to a person's self-esteem. Without our getting too "shrink-like," threats to self-esteem can be very frightening and unconscious, and they can generate a high degree of anxiety.

In Susan's case, you could imagine that she experienced an uncomfortable degree of anxiety when her supervisor threatened her belief that she was a completely valuable and competent worker. In Susan's case, not unlike many Sealed PITAs, she interpreted the questioning of her work behaviors as a personal attack. She generalized a couple of comments about her workplace performance to the larger context of her functioning as a human being. As a result, the degree of threat was substantial to Susan, whereas it would be less intense to someone who did not make these types of assumptions.

To fully understand the nature of Susan's defensiveness, you'd have to delve into a very complicated process reserved for the work of good therapists. The answer probably lies somewhere in her past jobs, past relationships, or even current life circumstances. As a professional in the workplace, however, you are not responsible for playing the role of therapist to your supervisees, coworkers, or superiors. The best you can do is to intervene calmly, consistently, and professionally by pointing out the defensiveness and encouraging a more honest evaluation of the behaviors in question. It also helps to understand that defense reactions are to a degree shared by everyone. No one is exempt from feeling defensive about at least one aspect of his or her self or life.

Stuck Personalities

From the interaction with Susan, there were some signs that corrective interactions with her might not be easy or necessarily straightforward. Recall that the earlier confrontation by the Director of Nursing was met with defensiveness, tearful agitation, and turning the tables on the DON by becoming the victim. It would have been greatly helpful to Susan if she could have maintained a nondefense stance when confronted about her less-than-professional behavior. As is so often the case with a Sealed PITA, efforts to get at the core issue or core problem are frustrating, time-consuming, and typically let go in the end.

Defensive patterns of behaviors are learned over time, and sometimes no intervention—no matter how delicately presented— can create inroads for change or improvement. M. Scott Peck addressed this very theme in his most controversial book *People of the Lie* (1983), in which he presented case after case of people who committed very destructive interpersonal and psychological acts and lived in complete denial of their impact on the people they profoundly influenced and typically harmed. In many cases, these destructive behaviors were targeted toward family members who they supposedly loved and not just toward people in the workplace. As a talented psychiatrist who had years of experience with confronting destructive behavior, Dr. Peck also realized that he could have little impact on some people with very sealed personalities. Although he didn't use the term "Sealed PITA," his references to People of the Lie explained a very similar concept: the inability of some people to honestly look at themselves and all the personal motivations, unmet needs, fears, and early life forces that dominate behavior.

Strategies for Coping with a Sealed PITA

Intervening with a Sealed PITA is no easy task because it is understood that changes can occur only if the person acknowledges that change needs to happen. If the PITA will not acknowledge his or her responsibility and the unwanted behaviors continue, you may have to enlist the help of a supervisor or manager. Ideally, some interventions can take place before the person becomes a true PITA and disciplinary action is the only recourse.

When Your Direct Report Is a Sealed PITA: Tips for Managers

- Be emotionally even and hold your ground when you provide feedback to your direct report. It's likely that you will get a defensive reaction in the beginning.

(continued)

(continued)

- Make recommendations for improvements instead of just emphasizing the negative behavior. A positive tone creates more openings with a Sealed PITA than a critical tone.

- Be sure to document specific behaviors and interactions. Because Sealed PITAs frequently won't admit wrongdoing, you may need concrete documentation.

Create a Spirit of Trust

The calm, empathic, nonjudging approach can often soften a Sealed PITA and create possibilities for openings. If the DON had built trust with Susan and the perceptions of personal threat were altered, Susan might have been able to actually hear and "let in" some of the feedback. She might have been able to make some interventions on her own that would improve her workplace attitude and behaviors.

It's important to note here that we are not relieving the DON of her responsibility for holding Susan accountable. We are merely trying to optimize her interpersonal style and method of delivery for offering feedback. Of course, generating trust can be complicated in that it depends on whether Susan in fact trusts her supervisor enough to receive and really listen to her constructive critical feedback. Many employees do not trust the person to whom they report, for a variety of reasons. This is why it is important for you, as a supervisor, to be viewed as a person of fairness and integrity.

Be Collaborative

It's important to adopt a position of collaboration as opposed to a position of authority. The directive, authoritarian approach will only put a coworker or employee more on the defensive. You'll lose any chance of finding an opening and having a productive conversation. Openings are generally created through a spirit of understanding, empathy, and a focus on the positive. In our scenario, it might have helped to ask Susan for her own opinion about her work performance, about not showing up due to snow, or about helping out under emergency circumstances or in certain situations when the nursing team needs special assistance.

Often you can make more progress in these types of situations if you hold off on your opinion or perspective until the person in question gets his or her chance to respond, explain, or clarify. If a person is characteristically sealed, unsealing is usually best done by that person and not by you.

Emphasize Positives First

Another effective intervention in coping with a Sealed PITA is to begin on a positive note. Some acknowledgment of Susan's positive work behaviors would be very important to mention in the beginning of the conversation, such as her accuracy in medication management, her ethical attention to patient care, or any other characteristics identified by her supervisor.

The DON did in fact start out the conversation by pointing out that Susan had been a good nurse in terms of her clinical skills, that she was respected for her patient care, and that she was valued for many reasons. It might also be helpful to acknowledge Susan's concern about missing work due to snow and mention that bad weather does pose driving difficulties and create more stress.

Ideally, Susan would recognize that this assessment of her work performance is not a personal attack and that her Director of Nursing is capable of seeing the positives of her performance and not just focusing on negative behaviors.

Comment on Specific Behaviors and Not the Person

It's important to be clear and precise when addressing performance problems and keep the focus on specific behaviors. Recall that the DON focused on the problem areas. She said that there were some behaviors (for example, not pitching in during critical situations) that were not professional and that these behaviors were the source of concern.

Notice that the DON did not say that Susan herself was not professional. She said that Susan displayed some behaviors that were not professional. This type of intervention helps make it clear that Susan as a person is not the problem, so that Susan doesn't then become immediately defensive. Almost always, references to specific behaviors only rather than a person in general can lead to more positive results. However, even if you do everything correctly, don't expect the Sealed PITA to come around immediately. The interaction between the DON and Susan is an example of how these conversations typically start out, but it's important to stay the course. Susan may begin to take an honest look at her behaviors later after the threat and discomfort of the initial confrontation are over.

Appreciate What the Sealed PITA Brings to the Table

It's important to take a balanced look at the Sealed PITA and acknowledge that there are some aspects of being sealed that are functional. When you are sealed, you have a high degree of resiliency and you are able to deflect threatening criticisms. Being sealed can keep you safe from other PITAs out there in the world. Your sealed tendencies particularly offer good protection against those folks with Crusty, Overstuffed, and some Combo PITA styles. There is such a thing as a healthy amount of sealed-ness.

Professionals Increasing Their Awareness: Strategies for Becoming Less Sealed

Whether you're a seasoned professional, a new hire, or someone seeking employment, keep an eye on your own potential to become a Sealed PITA. Few behaviors will annoy your supervisors, coworkers, and employees more than the fact that you cannot demonstrate some degree of self-awareness and take personal responsibility for your attitudes, work relationships, and performance. "What a pain in the ass" is not a comment that you want popping into people's heads or whispered about you when you leave the room. Unfortunately, most Sealed PITAs have no idea that they are Sealed PITAs.

Here are some suggestions and strategies for minimizing your potential for being a Sealed PITA.

Engage in Honest Reflection

The process of looking inward and being honest with yourself is difficult but necessary. In this chapter's work scenario, it's up to Susan to listen, absorb some of the feedback, and consider what might be happening with her as it pertains to her problematic work behaviors. This period of honest reflection might happen immediately while engaged in the discussion, or it might require chewing on the information and processing it for a couple of days so that issues have time to settle. But in the end, something has to be absorbed and owned. This is the only path to self-improvement and overcoming the personal barriers that keep us stuck in ineffective behaviors.

If honest reflection can happen, real discussion could follow and the problems could be seen more clearly. Perhaps Susan did not like her job very much and she was making any excuse possible not to be at the nursing facility. Maybe she was having a problem with a coworker and she was avoiding that particular person, resulting in her tendency to bolt out the door whenever her shift was over. It might be that on a global level she just really believed that being a team player was not that important and that pitching in beyond her regular duties was not a crucial job function. Regardless of the reason, at least honest reflection and real conversation could occur so that both parties could get at the core of the problem (or problems).

Stay Open to the Idea That Everyone Has Strengths and Growth Areas

A primary characteristic of the most valuable employees in any organization is that they are open to challenging themselves by honestly and openly acknowledging their deficits. No employees ever got better by just accepting their most positive features. In order to excel, workers have to be able to own their weakest areas, too. There are countless famous athletes, entertainers, and businesspeople who began their professions with deficits to address and overcome.

The sport of gymnastics is an example of an endeavor that requires its athletes to work on many aspects of themselves in order to be ready for competition. To be the best at their game, gymnasts do not have the luxury of being strong in just one event while neglecting others. They understand that they must be just as strong in the parallel bars and balance beam as they are in their floor exercise. Think of these athletes as just another kind of worker with strengths and weaknesses to be addressed.

Understand That No One Is Perfect: Embrace Your Imperfections

Understanding that no one is perfect might seem counterintuitive, since we are trying to get you to become better at self-awareness. The truth is that there is a paradox regarding Sealed PITA behavior. The more you *need* to be perfect, the less willing you are to be open to your growth areas. One of the characteristics of a person who suffers from pathological perfectionism is that he or she cannot tolerate being flawed or, worse yet, having people actually see that he or she has flaws. To accept the fundamental human quality of being flawed is terribly anxiety-provoking to Sealed PITAs, so they will defend against any evidence that they are not perfect.

The best way to become open to your weaknesses (growth areas) and to feedback is to work to become more accepting of yourself as an imperfect human being. The best way to begin this process is through changing the way you talk to yourself. Yes, we all talk to ourselves! Developing a calm internal voice that is forgiving when you are less than perfect is a good start. If you have an internal voice that berates you when you mess up or when you are not 100 percent, give it a chill pill.

Regularly Seek Feedback Regarding Workplace Performance

One requirement of doctoral programs that train students of counseling psychology is that students meet weekly with a supervisor to discuss their performance as budding clinicians. This serves a twofold purpose of offering regular constructive feedback to students with the goal of improving their clinical work while also giving them practice at looking at themselves with a critical eye and developing their ability to be self-corrective.

A similar process can and should take place with working professionals. Regular meetings or conversations with a trusted coworker, supervisor, or mentor can create opportunities to become a better and more valuable employee. The conversations conducted repeatedly over time can also desensitize you to the initial discomfort associated with revealing deficits to another person. Repetition tends to ease the sting and make you more open to your growth areas.

Take Some Risks and Try Things That Are Hard and Different

A valued colleague is a master at taking interpersonal risks. He is able to courageously place himself into the uncomfortable situations that most of us avoid. He enthusiastically takes on public-speaking engagements, he freely makes fun of himself in public (which people find endearing), and he brings levity and humor into situations in which the mood is serious and the attendees self-important. The beauty of his uninhibited behavior is that he pulls it off. How?

The answer is largely that he is honest with himself about his strengths and shortcomings and he is not afraid to fail. He's the first to admit that he is not the brightest guy, that he is not particularly articulate, and that he does not like his physical appearance. Yet, he fearlessly "puts himself out there" in ways that demonstrate self-confidence way beyond that exhibited by most gifted men. We mention this colleague because he is the complete opposite of the Sealed PITA in that he welcomes feedback and is able to laugh at himself. As a result, he makes ongoing self-improvements and he tackles difficult tasks.

CHAPTER 3

The Crusty PITA:
A Negative, Grouchy Coworker

Most people buy a pita sandwich because of its soft texture and fresh taste. There aren't many pita eaters out there who want a stale, crusty pita. It's not fun trying to eat a crusty pita; as it crumbles and falls apart, you become increasingly annoyed and frustrated, finally deciding to throw away the last few broken pieces. After feeling dissatisfied with the pita you just ate, you vow to yourself that the next time you eat a pita, you'll do everything you can to avoid getting a hard, crusty one.

Likewise in the working world, not too many people out there want to work with a crusty, negative, grouchy coworker. Nobody enjoys being around a coworker who complains about everything and everybody, who cuts down every new idea and every accomplishment, who talks negatively about people behind their backs, and who blames others when things don't go his or her way. Just as people in a food market try hard to avoid buying a crusty pita, people in the world of work try hard to avoid interacting with a crusty pain in the ass.

A Working Definition for the Crusty PITA

A Crusty PITA is a coworker or employee who is negative, cynical, mean-spirited, grouchy, and pessimistic, and who sees the glass as half-empty. Throughout this

(continued)

(continued)

> chapter, we refer to these negative characteristics as the "crust" and people who display these characteristics as being "crusty." We'll also refer to those situations that tend to cause crusty behavior as "crusty situations."

The Crusty PITA at Work

Crusty PITAs show their faces in many different work situations: individual meetings, staff meetings, and committees (or project teams) to name a few. Because Crusty PITAs often rear their heads in committee meetings, the following scenario illustrates the dynamics of a Crusty PITA, Albert, as he serves on an office-wide committee trying to plan the year-end retreat.

Coworkers from 10 different work units were asked to serve on the Retreat Planning Committee. In forming this committee, the CEO was hoping to get a diversity of perspectives to shape the retreat in a healthy way, receive "buy-in" across work units, and build team morale across work units.

Albert, an accountant, doesn't get out much, and that's just fine by him. He generally feels that socials and retreats are a waste of time and money. His supervisor, Allie, thought that it would be good for Albert to mix with some colleagues from other departments. So she asked Albert to serve on the committee.

Famous Crusty PITAs

Here are some characters from popular television shows and movies who exemplify Crusty PITA characteristics:

- Henry Fonda as Norman Thayer *(On Golden Pond)*

- Edward Asner as Lou Grant *(The Mary Tyler Moore Show)*

- Leslie David Baker as Stanley Hudson *(The Office)*

- Peter Boyle as Frank Barone *(Everybody Loves Raymond)*

- Roseanne Barr as Roseanne Conner *(Roseanne)*

- Vic Tayback as Mel Sharples *(Alice)*

- Danny DeVito as Louie De Palma *(Taxi)*

- Ed O'Neill as Al Bundy *(Married with Children)*

- Sherman Hemsley as George Jefferson *(The Jeffersons)*

During the first committee meeting, the other members began brainstorming ideas for the year-end retreat. Everything from boat races to bowling to pig roasts was put on the table as possible retreat activities. There was a lot of creative, positive energy surrounding the discussion. Albert sat quietly, looking down most of the time. Finally, near the end of the meeting, one of the members asked Albert what he thought, and Albert replied, "I don't see how any of this will help us improve as a company. I think our hard-earned money could be spent on more useful things than pig roasts and rowboats. Why don't they spend that money to pay us better?"

When the meeting ended, Albert quickly returned to his office to get back to work. One of Albert's coworkers, Randy, asked him how the meeting went. Albert replied, "It was a waste of my time. I could have gotten my report done, but instead I had to listen to a bunch of blowhards talk about bowling and pig roasts. It's amazing that we don't have money for a better copier, but we can rent out the entire bowling alley for everybody. If we go through with this, I'm going to give our CEO a piece of my mind, 'cause this is a waste of money!"

After Albert arbitrarily blew off the second and third planning meetings, the Retreat Committee Chairperson called Allie to see whether Albert would be joining the committee for the next meeting. Allie was angry with Albert, feeling as though he was disrespectful to her and the work unit by taking it upon himself to blow off the meetings. She confronted Albert in his office, demanding an explanation. Albert responded, "I have a pile of work that has to get done. I don't have time to be planning pig roasts."

Allie shut the office door and gave Albert a tongue lashing, explaining that he represents their entire work unit and that his decision not to attend the meetings made the whole unit look bad. Allie stormed out of the office after laying out clear expectations to attend the remaining committee meetings. Albert sat with his head down and didn't say anything.

Feeling the need to vent, Albert went over to Randy's desk and verbally blasted Allie behind her back, stating that she's "an idiot who has to kiss the CEO's butt all the time." Randy, a younger and newer employee, tries to avoid Albert's frequent tirades, but it's easier said than done. He doesn't want to make any waves, so he chooses to listen neutrally. But lately Albert has started to get to him. He's uncomfortable with how loud Albert is at times and is afraid other coworkers will overhear him blasting Allie. Randy recently began talking to his wife about Albert, wondering what he should do about the situation.

Albert unwillingly attended the remaining three meetings, sitting quietly with a scowl on his face. He went through the motions and did as little as possible, while never volunteering or initiating any thoughts or ideas. Without his input, the committee eventually decided to go with the boat race idea.

During the retreat, Allie had a chance to talk to the chairperson of the retreat committee regarding Albert's participation. Not surprisingly, the chairperson didn't speak favorably about Albert's attitude and involvement. Allie shook her head and flailed her arms in disgust. Albert's behavior and attitude put a damper on what should have been a fun and rewarding day for her and everyone else.

Understanding the Crusty PITA

Before you try to figure out how to work with such a negative coworker, it's helpful to understand Crusty PITAs a little better. By far, the most important thing to remember when dealing with Crusty PITAs is this:

You cannot take personally the things they say or do!

Crusty PITAs growl at the world and everything around them. As you saw in the scenario, Albert looks for flaws in people and things to complain about. It was probably a Crusty PITA who created the phrase "seeing the glass half-empty." They have a chip on their shoulder and an anger inside, ready to lash out at any point in time. To truly understand the source of the anger and crust, you would need a skilled therapist. There are so many possible explanations or reasons why they've become crusty that you'll probably never really know how your particular crusty coworkers got that way. So it won't be very useful trying to figure out why.

Reasons for Crustiness

It is, however, useful to have a general understanding of some of the possible explanations as to how people become crusty.

Realizing that there are usually factors out of crusty coworkers' control that are causing the crust might give you a bit more sympathy and tolerance when interacting with your crusty coworkers.

Born Crusty

One cluster of possible explanations focuses on innate reasons. As we know from psychology, people are born with a distinct personality and temperament. Maybe your crusty coworker was simply born with a crusty personality or temperament. And personality normally doesn't change over time or through the aging process.

In their renowned research (*Temperament and Development*, 1977), psychiatrists Thomas and Chess reported that, as people age, their temperament stays the same. It simply deepens over the years. Most people don't know, for example, that the "grumpy old man" syndrome is really just a myth. A gentle and kind old man was probably a gentle and kind young man. Conversely, a grumpy, crusty old man was probably a grumpy, crusty young man.

Made Crusty by Bad Experiences

A second cluster of possible explanations stems from one's upbringing and childhood. When a person experiences emotional or verbal abuse from important people in his or her life, or if these important people model crusty behavior, this person is likely to form somewhat of a thick crust himself or herself. If a person's peers or friends constantly put down or bullied him or her when growing up, he or she might have built up resentment and might "act out" in crusty ways.

Crusty Because of a Lack of Self-Esteem

Another cluster of possible explanations has to do with how one sees oneself, or one's self-esteem. Those who didn't experience much success in school, sports, or social activities, for example, might view themselves as failures. Some people don't like the way they look and are jealous of others who are more attractive. Others might be jealous of people whom they see as more successful.

Although these perceptions may not necessarily be true, it's their way of viewing others that's the problem. These insecurities that lead to low self-esteem can cause crusty people to want to look for inadequacies in others. They put others down in an unhealthy attempt to feel better about themselves (misery loves company).

Again, there are a whole host of possible reasons why your crusty coworker is the way that he or she is. Try to be somewhat sympathetic toward him or her; it's not a fun way to go through life.

Situational Crustiness

Of course, there are varying degrees and frequencies of Crusty PITAs. Some are in your face, dishing out verbal jabs throughout every day. Others are less direct (they talk behind your back) and have hang-ups related only to certain things. Albert's hang-ups were social events at the office and spending money on morale-building functions.

Some Crusty PITAs show their ugly face to everybody, whereas others show it to only a select few. Notice that Albert expressed his "crust" most easily with his younger colleague, Randy, yet he was more closed-mouthed with his boss, Allie. Albert felt safer letting Randy see his crust because Randy wasn't in a position to evaluate or reprimand him. When it came to the Retreat Planning Committee, Albert rode the fence. Because he didn't know his colleagues from other units very well, he held in his anger and resentment until he was asked to offer his opinion. When given the green light to speak, Albert let out his anger and revealed his true colors.

Strategies for Coping with a Crusty PITA

Now that you understand Crusty PITAs a little better, you're in a better position to cope more effectively as you encounter them in the workplace. Following are several strategies for working more effectively with the Crusty PITA.

Rise Above It

The worst thing that can happen is that the crust starts rubbing off on you. Just as we preach to our kids how critical it is to be your own person and not to be influenced by the "wrong crowd," it's important that you don't succumb to the crust and fall into the Crusty PITA's half-empty glass.

This actually happens more than you might think. Haven't you ever found yourself venting along with a crusty coworker on a rainy Monday morning or after your boss came down on you? Come on, I'm sure you can remember a time or two when this happened. It's no "biggie" if you let yourself indulge once in a while—it can be therapeutic. But when you find yourself complaining more often about things or people you used to not complain about, it might be time to take a long look in the office bathroom mirror to see if the crust is getting a bit too thick for your liking.

Crust can be contagious. Many more times than not, as your Crusty PITA tries to lure you in, you need to rise above it. In the scenario, Randy, the young coworker who shared an office with Albert, was doing what he could to rise above it. Increasingly, Randy was bothered by Albert's tirades, which is a good sign. If you find yourself enjoying your negative coworker's tirades and frequent venting, you might be heading down the wrong path.

Don't Enable or Encourage

How many times have you heard parents say, after watching their child ham it up, "please don't encourage him"? Similarly, you owe it to your office and your company not to encourage the behavior of a Crusty PITA. At the very least, be neutral. Even the slightest, most subtle smirk may be all the reinforcement that a lonely Crusty PITA needs to keep verbally blasting another coworker.

Depending on your relationship and comfort level, consider gently challenging your angry coworker's views. For example, in our scenario, when Albert came back from the first planning meeting stating how ridiculous an idea boating is for the retreat, Randy could have gently challenged Albert's view by saying something like, "I think boating would be a fun way to get to know some of our colleagues better. Plus, I sure could use a day out of the office!"

Don't Write Them Off

In an attempt to "rise above it" and "keep from enabling," it's tempting to simply avoid contact with a Crusty PITA and write him or her off as a jerk or a waste of time. Out of basic humanity alone, we could never encourage you to write somebody off. Because Albert has offended coworkers, many of them have taken his crusty remarks personally and thus consider him a jerk who is not worth their time. That's a natural reaction. As more and more people avoid contact with him, the Crusty PITA feels increasingly alienated. This can only make him feel and act even more crusty.

I know it's asking a lot of you to not just avoid him. This is a test of your character: Adversity creates an opportunity to see what you're made of. It's easy to be friendly with the nice coworkers with whom you "click." It's tough to be warm and friendly toward the Crusty PITAs. Crusty PITAs might not show it, but they feel things, too. They certainly know when you haven't given up on them. Only those who keep trying have a chance to get through that crusty shell and make a difference.

When Your Direct Report Is a Crusty PITA: Tips for Managers

- Nip the crust in the bud when it's directed at you. If you allow your crusty direct report to talk to you in a disrespectful way, you are essentially giving him or her the green light to throw crust around on everybody else in the office. Don't enable this unhealthy behavior. It could become contagious.

- Model a firm yet crust-less approach when confronting your crusty direct report. Although you might feel inclined to use your position of power to put your crusty employee in his or her place by giving the employee a taste of his or her own (crusty) medicine, take the high road and lead by example, showing your report firsthand that you can be firm yet tactful when addressing serious issues with coworkers.

- Show your crusty employee that you still care about him or her. Even though it's natural not to feel as warmly toward a crusty employee as you do toward a friendly employee, don't quit on your crusty direct report. Your job as a manager is to get the most out of *all* of your employees, and it's difficult to get much out of an employee when he or she feels as though you could care less about

him or her. It's easy to forget that even crusty
employees have feelings inside and a need for
approval.

Pick Your Battles

As you work with a Crusty PITA, you need to establish some
boundaries to help determine which behaviors you can live with
and which behaviors you need to address in some manner. Much
of this depends on the working relationship you have with the
Crusty PITA. Obviously, if you're the supervisor, it's your
responsibility to help shape and evaluate the Crusty PITA's
behavior and performance. Thus, your boundary lines will be a bit
tighter and closer.

If you're a coworker working alongside a Crusty PITA, you are
not *required* to address or help shape his or her behavior. At times,
however, the Crusty PITA might cross a line, which forces you to
act.

Finally, if your supervisor is a Crusty PITA, your boundary lines
might look much different. With the type of relationship in mind,
assess the impact that the Crusty PITA's behavior is having on the
productivity, teamwork, and morale within your unit and company and determine whether you need to take any action.
Although you should continue to "rise above it," "remain positive," and "keep trying" as recommended in preceding coping
strategies, at times you will need to confront the Crusty PITA or
address your concerns to a third party. Pick your battles wisely!

Confront the Crusty PITA Individually

There will be times when you've tried everything—rising above,
gently challenging, remaining friendly—but nothing has helped,

and things are getting worse. You're at the point where you must do something. You can either confront the Crusty PITA directly, or you can share your concerns with your supervisor or an appropriate colleague.

Unless it's simply impossible, give the Crusty PITA the benefit of the doubt and address your concerns directly with him or her. More often than not, when you approach the Crusty PITA one on one, you'll find that his bark is much worse than his bite. It's common for Crusty PITAs to lash out without thinking and to be more aggressive with people who are passive and least resistant. But when they are challenged head on, the crust usually crumbles.

When addressing your concerns, treat the Crusty PITA with as much respect as you would any other colleague. Try not to put him or her on the defensive. Explain why you felt you needed to bring up this issue now, and that you want to see him or her succeed (show that you care). Of course, as a last resort, you might need to consult with a supervisor if the Crusty PITA's behaviors escalate when confronted.

Seek Out Positive Colleagues

One of the best ways to cope with a Crusty PITA is to hang out with fun, positive colleagues as much as possible. Join committees that consist of different colleagues to get away from the crust and build new working relationships. Establish weekly or biweekly lunches with colleagues who are more upbeat and positive.

From our PITA scenario, Randy began talking to his wife about Albert to help alleviate some of his growing frustration. Although talking to a family member about workplace challenges is fine, it can start dampening your personal time at home. Alleviating some of the frustration at work with colleagues can help you keep your work stuff at the office. With that said, be careful not to vent too frequently to your colleagues about your Crusty PITA—two wrongs don't make a right.

Appreciate What the Crusty PITA Brings to the Table

Coping with PITA coworkers is sometimes easier when you acknowledge some of their positive assets. Even the Crusty PITA has some positive things to offer. In a world of "walking on eggshells" and being politically correct, it can be refreshing at times to work with coworkers who say it how they see it. Our society has conditioned people to view blunt and direct communication as rude and callous. But sometimes it's nice to know that when Crusty PITAs talk, they're being 100 percent genuine regarding how they actually feel about a certain issue or topic. You might not always like what you see, but at least you can be assured that, when interacting with crusty coworkers, "what you see is what you get!"

Professionals Increasing Their Awareness: Strategies for Becoming Less Crusty

Everybody has moments of being a bit on edge, feeling crabby, and taking it out on others. As discussed earlier in the chapter, there are varying degrees of "crustiness." Some people get crusty only occasionally when somebody hits a nerve. Others are crusty all the time for seemingly no reason. No matter where you fall on the crustiness continuum, you always have room for improvement.

Following are strategies for increasing your self-awareness and keeping your own Crusty PITA tendencies in check.

Determine When You Are Most Likely to Be Crusty

A good place to start is to increase your awareness of those work or personal situations that tend to bring out the crust in you. Is it during certain functions or events (for example, staff meetings)? Is it when you are interacting with a particular coworker who gets under your skin? Is it a certain day of the week or time of the day? You might be grumpy in the morning or hate Mondays. Is it when you are discussing a sensitive topic that you feel passionately about, and a colleague takes the opposing side? For example, some people get very crusty when talking about politics or religion. Do you tend to be crusty when you've been experiencing a personal or family problem that you bring into work?

Find Out What's Beneath the Crust

Once you have determined *when* your potential for being crusty is highest, it's healthy to look beneath the surface and figure out *why* you get so crusty in these situations. What is it that gets you so stirred up and in such a crusty mood? Through challenging yourself like this, you might realize that you're projecting onto your coworkers your anger from something that took place years ago and has nothing to do with them. Increasing your awareness of what's causing the crust can help you channel your crust in more appropriate ways.

Create a New Recipe for Softening the Crust

Now that you have a better grasp on when and why the crust comes out, you can begin thinking about ways to "soften the crust" during those situations that tend to bring out the Crusty PITA in you. Is there an adjustment you can make in those crusty situations that enables you to behave or interact in a more positive way? For example, if you tend to "hit below the belt" when debating with colleagues on politics, think about how you could argue in a way that gets your point across strongly without offending others. If you come up with constructive, tactful "talking points" for topics that get you heated up, it could help soften the crust of your arguments.

Maybe your crust comes out when you interact with a certain coworker. Again, try to find a new recipe for dealing with that coworker. We tend to fall into habits of communicating with certain colleagues, with some interactions more tense than others. What can you do to break the negative communication habits that you have with certain colleagues?

Have Your "Crust Antenna" Up at All Times

Although you can anticipate and prepare for most crusty situations, there will always be those that come up out of the blue and catch you off guard. You need to have your "crust antenna" up at all times, heightening your awareness to crusty situations and helping you recognize when you're starting to get worked up. You need to be able to catch yourself before you start throwing your crust around.

In this chapter's PITA scenario, if Albert were more aware of his tendency to become annoyed at coworkers when discussing social events, he could have caught himself before he lashed out and maybe responded a bit more tactfully. I know what you're thinking: Albert probably doesn't care that he acts like a Crusty PITA. That's a whole different and more complex problem to overcome. But let's assume that you *do* care about keeping your crust in check. Knowing that you're entering a situation that usually brings out your crusty edge (increased awareness), and catching yourself when you're about to showcase that crusty edge, puts you in a favorable position to make a positive change.

Let Colleagues in on Your Crusty Tendencies

For those colleagues with whom you're comfortable, let them in on your crusty tendencies to help lessen the blow during crusty situations. Explaining to colleagues why you tend to get crusty can increase their understanding and help keep your working relationship intact.

This "letting colleagues in" can happen before or after crusty situations. For example, if you anticipate some crusty behavior on your part due to an upcoming period of long hours at work, you may ask certain colleagues to "bear with me" during this challenging time. On the other hand, after crusty situations have occurred, it's not too late to explain your crusty behavior to certain colleagues whom you believe deserve an explanation. Just don't fall into the pattern of always apologizing later. Next time, try to rein in your crustiness before it comes out.

Keep Work in Perspective

One of the ways to keep your crust in check is to simply keep work in perspective. What about your job is so important that it gets you all worked up and on edge? It's unfortunate that it takes a serious life tragedy like the death of somebody we know or seeing a child in a wheelchair to remind ourselves to keep things in perspective. Save your emotional energy for your family and friends.

That doesn't mean you shouldn't be passionate about your work. You should try to maintain a strong desire and positive attitude at work; just don't go overboard. If you truly believe that your job and the work atmosphere are responsible for making you crusty on a daily basis, it's probably time to start evaluating other options or changes to your work life. Keeping work in perspective might help your crust soften over time.

CHAPTER 4

The Overstuffed PITA:
A Full-of-Himself Glory Hound

E very organization has a few Overstuffed PITAs who usually occupy the upper ranks of the unit, department, or organization. Think of a pita that just can't fit any more "fixins" into its tight pocket without busting wide open. That should give you a mental picture of the Overstuffed PITA in the workplace. This is the person who is driven by being *more* and having *more*. Replace the "fixins" in abundance (the lettuce, tomatoes, pickles, peppers, mayo, and olives) with recognition, appreciation, credit, glory, money, promotions, and power, and you get the idea of what fills the overstuffed PITA. This is the person who seemingly can never get enough of whatever the workplace provides in terms of rewards and recognition.

The ultimate problem with the Overstuffed PITA is the fact that by being so into his or her own pursuit of more status, power, and attention, he or she often sacrifices the ability to look out for the well-being of the team. At their worst, Overstuffed PITAs consciously hold back other people for the sake of self-promotion. At their best, they are just oblivious to the fact that they hog the glory and that their appetites can keep other people from getting their piece of the recognition pie.

Again, it's common for an Overstuffed PITA to hold or to aspire to a position of power because ultimately this has been one of his or her primary driving forces. Positions of power come with other benefits that the Overstuffed PITA craves, so we often find such people in high-visibility positions across all types of business organizations, politics, and the media.

A Working Definition for the Overstuffed PITA

An Overstuffed PITA is a coworker who is self-absorbed, attention hungry, conceited, and aggressively self-promoting. Throughout this chapter, we refer to the people who display these characteristics as being "overstuffed." We also refer to those situations that tend to cause overstuffed behavior as "overstuffed situations."

The Overstuffed PITA at Work

Consider this example of a young man well on his way to becoming an Overstuffed PITA. Ben was a young professional just out of law school, with an eye toward making his mark on the legal world. Like so many young attorneys, he had his sights set on the big-money, high-profile life of becoming a partner in a large urban law firm. In fact, he was recruited aggressively by a major New York firm specializing in corporate law. He was ultimately hired with a handsome salary and bonus package.

Ben came from a family of high-profile professionals. His father was a respected neurosurgeon and his mother was an ambitious corporate attorney. He received messages from very early on that achievement was the number-one priority. So he responded with exceptional grades all through high school and college, and received other accolades as a gifted debater and athlete. Ben was admitted into an Ivy League college, where he double-majored in international politics and biology, two demanding areas of study that left room for few electives.

Ben was not really sure why he chose the two majors, other than the fact that they would provide solid preparation for a career in business, law, or medicine, three prestigious and typically well-paid professions. He could not make clear distinctions about why one might be a better choice for him in terms of his interests, values, or skills. All that mattered to him was that the final outcome was entering a profession of distinction with high earning potential.

Ben was also involved in many clubs in college, his motivation being that ultimately they would look good on his resume and would impress potential employers or graduate schools. He did apply to and got accepted by a respectable number of high-caliber law schools. He chose to attend the one with the best reputation for getting its graduates the highest starting salaries after graduation.

From reading Ben's background and aspirations thus far, you might feel a degree of respect, or even admiration, for this high-achieving young man. But this is where the story unravels for Ben. People in his work and personal life really did not care for Ben, a young professional on the fast track. He did not develop much of a social life other than those rare times when there was a formal work function or office party where everyone was invited. Rarely did another person or group invite him to hang out, have dinner, or go to a movie. Ben was just not a hanging-out, easygoing kind of guy.

Famous Overstuffed PITAs

Here are some characters from popular television shows and movies who exemplify Overstuffed PITA characteristics:

- Michael J. Fox as Alex P. Keaton *(Family Ties)*

- Kelsey Grammer as Dr. Frasier Crane *(Cheers/Frasier)*

- Larry Hagman as John Ross "J. R." Ewing, Jr. *(Dallas)*

- Calista Flockhart as Kitty Walker *(Brothers and Sisters)*

- Greg Germann as Richard Fish *(Ally McBeal)*

- Simon Cowell as himself *(American Idol: The Search for a Superstar)*

- Henry Winkler as Arthur "Fonzie" Fonzarelli *(Happy Days)*

- Jay Mohr as Bob Sugar *(Jerry Maguire)*

- Will Ferrell as Chazz Michael Michaels *(Blades of Glory)*

In conversations, Ben tended to dominate and overwhelm people. He had little idea about the notion of reciprocity of exchange, in which two people who are engaged in a conversation understand that there is some sort of balance between talk time and listening time. Ben saw conversation times as occasions when he could talk about himself, glorify his accomplishments, minimize the accomplishments of other people, and "talk at" his more passive partner. He overwhelmed people's ears. He quickly rerouted back to himself moments when other people had the floor, dictating the conversation and talking about himself. People felt as if he were barely listening when it came time for them to have their turn to speak. A typical conversation with Ben might go like this:

Ben's colleague Sara: "Hey, Ben, did you hear that I've been doing some pro bono work for one of the local social service agencies? I know it doesn't pay anything, but it makes me feel like I'm offering something back to the community, ya know?"

Ben: "I used to do some pro bono work at one time, and I did some really good work. I actually won a few cases that would have put a couple of those places out of business but I saved them. They asked me to keep representing them but I just knew my time was more valuable than working for free so I gave it up. They still call me from time to time because they know that the guy they are using now is just not as good."

Sara: "Well, I'm glad that I decided to represent this agency because they do a lot of positive work for women in the neighborhood and they need good counsel now and then. I feel good that I can help them out. It doesn't take all that much time for the amount of assistance they really need."

Ben: "Wow, you should have seen all the work that I did for this one nonprofit agency down in the city. I must have heard from them every week, wanting me to advise them on the most trivial issues. I hope the group you are representing is not nearly as demanding because, boy, it can be a real hassle. I remember this one case that took me an outrageous number of hours to prepare for. I mean I won the case and all because the other attorneys weren't real sharp—they missed many of the key details in the case. I have always been a thorough researcher, so I immediately knew where to strike when it came time to go to court."

On a number of levels, this exchange between Ben and Sara demonstrates his Overstuffed PITA tendencies. First, he did not really respond to Sara's news as if he was really listening and understanding the satisfaction she was getting from her pro bono work. Second, he used her news to go off on his own story about a time when he did a similar kind of work. He might have been trying to identify with her, but he came off as self-serving. Third, he was always very quick to somehow interject that either someone really wanted him or that he was in some way very talented. He was good at tooting his own horn—although just a bit too blatantly.

Ben's group and committee work within the law firm often led to similar kinds of interactions. He was a capable decision maker with a rational mind and good ideas. However, he had trouble getting his colleagues to buy into his recommendations and approaches. Why so?

The answer lies somewhere in Ben's lack of awareness about the impact that he has on people in general and, in this case, on his legal team. Because time is money in the practice of law, it is widely acknowledged that meetings have to be focused and efficient. When Ben takes the lead, he appropriately starts meetings by suggesting that his team be sensitive to time and that individuals not take any more than their allotted share. Ordinarily, the standard is approximately 15 minutes per attorney, depending on the size of the cases and the number of cases to discuss.

Now, you would think that Ben would also follow his own expectations for being considerate and conserving time, right? Wrong! In the same breath that he tells people to stay aware of time, he launches into his own 30-minute monologues that are often filled with tangentially relevant material and personal anecdotes and impressions about a variety of issues. In essence, the meetings represent another opportunity for Ben to have the stage and "talk at" people.

So, as stated earlier, Ben encounters lots of resistance when trying to get his team to consider his ideas and approaches to legal matters. The interesting part is that it's not necessarily that his ideas are bad. He just irritates people and they become passive-aggressive and noncompliant.

This is where the problem gets even more complicated and what makes Ben most PITA-like and most in need of some awareness. Instead of going into problem-solving mode and asking himself why his legal teams resist his ideas and his approaches, Ben resorts to other rationalizations. He shifts responsibility to the people who are not on board with his plans. His reaction is often vindictive and bitter. Ben is a blamer. When someone disagrees with him, Ben gets angry and makes character assassinations on the other team members. His comments range from "he's just incompetent and not dedicated" to "she's a lightweight and not intellectual enough to be on the team." Worse yet, he makes these comments behind his colleagues' backs, not being aware enough to realize that these comments will ultimately get back to them.

Ben's PITA style could potentially hamper his career. With workplaces increasingly recognizing that interpersonal effectiveness and character are highly important qualities for effective leaders, the Overstuffed PITA like Ben needs to be more vigilant about avoiding team-damaging behaviors. Although the Overstuffed

PITA might be effective up to a certain point, high-level administrative positions that require managerial finesse and inter-personal sensitivity and competence will be filled by people who motivate their employees instead of deflating them.

Understanding the Overstuffed PITA

In Ben's case, he has taken on a personality style that is marked by constant needs for affirmation, adoration, and superiority over others. The problematic word here is "constant." It is quite func-tional to want to achieve individual competence and to master different life tasks. It feels good to experience the rush of leading a group to success, winning an athletic event, or expressing your-self in a way that has an impact on your listeners. Yet, in life, these external affirmations that make us feel great come only now and again, a real-life phenomenon that is insufficient for Ben's need for constant external strokes.

For Ben, the problem is twofold. First, his needs for all the "good stuff" were quite massive. Visualize the gaping pocket inside a pita sandwich that is busting wide open, yet never quite gets com-pletely filled because there's a tear in the bottom. Second, Ben has lost or never developed the capability to hold onto the good stuff long enough to see himself through a typical day or week where he does not need to be in the spotlight through entertaining, lead-ing, impressing, or manipulating another person. For whatever reason (which is the source of major debate among theorists and practitioners in psychology), Ben's tremendously engulfing needs are dictating his behaviors. For things to change, he needs to do some honest self-reflection or seek out the assistance of a trusted friend, family member, or professional to help him become more aware of the way he impacts others and to make the necessary changes in order to improve his relationships.

Understandably, most people who have to deal with Ben are not trained psychotherapists, nor should they put themselves in this position. However, the right caring, uncritical yet honest approach to Ben's behaviors could produce beneficial results. It is important to be aware of the common reactions that you might encounter when approaching Ben with any type of honest feedback about his behavior, potentially encompassing denial, anger, minimization, and blaming.

Strategies for Coping with an Overstuffed PITA

Intervening with or even coexisting with the Overstuffed PITA is quite a challenge. You're not a psychologist, so you can't aspire to change these PITAs' personalities yourself. However, there are strategies for coping with frustrating day-to-day interactions with an Overstuffed PITA

Stay Mindful of the Core Problem

It is always important to keep in mind that the core issue that drives the Overstuffed PITA is *insecurity*. In the scenario, Ben's insecurity about being successful enough, particularly given his parents' overemphasis on achievement, was his primary issue. He relied entirely on positive external re-enforcers such as position, attention, and adoration to make him feel okay. Ben was unable to derive much internally generated satisfaction about his quality as a worker or even a human being. In essence, he could feel good only if he was elevated by the people in his life thinking he was great.

As a colleague of an Overstuffed PITA, you might find it helpful to know that his or her behaviors are prompted by feelings of insecurity. This can help ease the frustration and anger that you often feel in the presence of this type of person. Knowing that deep down the Overstuffed PITA feels badly about himself or herself can help you keep in perspective the perceived threat to your own self-esteem that this person presents.

Be Realistic About Your Challenge with the Overstuffed PITA

In facing the challenge, we are drawn to the work of Drs. Aaron Beck and Arthur Freeman (1990), highly regarded psychologists who have written extensively on brief, cognitive approaches to conducting therapy with difficult personalities. They are realists when it comes to working with deeply ingrained personality styles; they realize that changing a personality is very difficult and that small successes are more the norm. To achieve these small successes, Beck and Freeman focus on helping their clients develop new attitudes by challenging their "faulty beliefs."

This practical and results-oriented approach focuses on changing the way people think (cognitions) about themselves in order to bring about changes in their behaviors. In Ben's case, he might think that he *always* has to be better than his colleagues to be appreciated and respected. An alternative belief that would serve Ben better would be that often it's okay to be *like* the others, rather than be *better* than the others. If Ben can learn to change this belief, he might not try so hard to be superior all the time.

Be Careful About Your Instant Reaction

The approach that you have to take with Overstuffed PITAs is to help them salvage their self-esteem as opposed to diminishing it. What does this mean? Our natural reaction to an Overstuffed

PITA's need to hog the attention, tendency to talk over people, reluctance to listen, and all the other time- and energy-sucking behaviors is to get angry.

It would feel great to let Ben have it, to one day blast him for all the times that he was self-absorbed and insensitive. In the moment, this might feel great and the built-up tension could be released in one giant tirade. It would be a short-term strategy for tension release and to put the PITA in his place, but it has little benefit as a long-term solution. The correct way of dealing with a person such as Ben is to approach specific concerns assertively, calmly, and in a way that doesn't threaten his self-esteem. Wow, what a challenge!

When Your Direct Report Is an Overstuffed PITA: Tips for Managers

- Overstuffed PITAs thrive on praise, so begin any discussion about performance improvements with some examples of their work that you appreciate.

- Explain that your feedback is designed to help them excel and make it clear that receptivity to your feedback might have payoffs down the road. Overstuffed PITAs tend to thrive on advancement and power, so be sure to point out the benefits of their cooperating.

- Remember that Overstuffed PITAs are more fragile than they appear. Don't respond too harshly just because their overstuffed demeanor suggests that they can handle it.

Confront Respectfully and Calmly

It's important to confront Overstuffed PITAs in a way that has some chance of eliciting the necessary changes to their thinking and behaviors. Of course, this all depends on the power relationship that you have with them—whether they are committee members, supervisors, subordinates, or friends. Still, some general guidelines hold true regardless.

Confront Overstuffed PITAs in a way that conveys respect for them as human beings. This approach is not about putting them in their place or putting them down. It's about generating an understanding that specific behaviors in which they engage are not working for you and the group and probably are not helping them reach their ultimate goals, either.

Address Behaviors That Are Specific and Current

Make feedback specific to the behaviors that are occurring in the present. If the Overstuffed PITA takes up too much time talking in meetings, make the feedback specific to that particular issue. A comment such as "It would be helpful to me if we could all, including you, stick to the proper allotted time. I understand that you have important information to communicate; however, it is frustrating for me when I feel rushed and my agenda is not fully communicated." Because you have made it clear that the PITA's time talking is important and that you are not dismissing him or her altogether, there is a better chance that the Overstuffed PITA will hear this feedback.

Use Concrete Examples

Be ready to provide examples of the point that you are trying to convey. Your opinion or your theory might not matter to

Overstuffed PITAs. They probably believe that they are superior to you in a multitude of ways, a rationalization they will use to minimize the importance of your feedback. To bolster the credibility of your feedback, provide some concrete examples of the behavior in question and the adverse results of the behavior.

Using Ben as the example, you could point out that his team members appear to respond negatively to his agenda when he is not considerate of their time because it communicates that their opinions are not as important as his. Citing an actual example of a specific meeting or series of meetings could help your cause. In addition, if you can in some way convey the message that you're providing this feedback because you want to see him succeed and that you care about Ben's success as an associate and ultimately partner, you might increase your chances of being taken seriously. Remember that being a partner is something that motivates him.

Be Prepared for Strong Reactions

Accept the fact that Overstuffed PITAs might not respond to your feedback in a way that immediately feels rewarding. No matter how skilled you are as a sensitive provider of delicate feedback, there is still a good chance that Overstuffed PITAs will initially be defensive. The PITAs may exhibit any one of a range of reactive behaviors. They might

- Fold their arms and seemingly close themselves off

- Look down as if embarrassed or shamed

- Deny that they engage in the behaviors of which you speak

- Appear agitated and verbally lash out

Regardless of the PITA's initial response, the fact that you have delivered your message in a thoughtful and meaningful way increases the chances that the Overstuffed PITA will digest the information in a way that has some impact. It may take a couple of hours or days to let his or her guard down enough to let in the information and fully consider your message. So you will have to let go of your own need for immediate gratification. You may also never really fully know whether your feedback made an impression because it's unlikely that the Overstuffed PITA will ever admit that you played a role in the change. It's much more likely that the Overstuffed PITA will claim that any positive changes are the result of his or her original ideas and not yours.

Consult with Trusted Peers

Discuss your approach with someone who knows the situation well in your organization. Obviously, the risk that you take with approaching a supervisor or someone in a position of power is much greater than approaching someone on your level or in a subordinate position. You'll need to consider many individual nuances. Sometimes a trusted coworker can help you practice your approach or provide good counsel about how to deal with your particular Overstuffed PITA.

Appreciate What the Overstuffed PITA Brings to the Table

Overstuffed qualities certainly have their place in most professions and work organizations. People with a good dose of overstuffedness are likely to be ambitious and capable. They tend to take responsibility and want to take the lead on projects. Most money-making organizations desire some overstuffed traits in many of their employees. Again, balancing these traits is a matter of degree and knowing when it's good to be stuffed and when it's best to unload some of your filling.

Professionals Increasing Their Awareness: Strategies for Becoming Less Overstuffed

Ben has extensive growth potential if he can manage to develop some awareness and insight into a few of the behaviors that are most toxic to other people. Ben's bridge from the PITA of the "Pain In The Ass" variety into the "Professionals Increasing Their Awareness" variety could mean the difference between a sub-par leader with reluctant followers and a skilled leader with willing and productive team members.

There is little doubt that Ben is intelligent, capable, and highly motivated. It's not an issue of his being more and doing more. In fact, the issue is really about doing less. The Chinese symbol of yin and yang can help illuminate Ben's struggle and need for balance. Yang can be viewed as the action side of life. It is purposeful and goal focused. It calls for planning, clear directives, and motion. Yin, on the other hand, calls for observation and passivity. It is the side of inactivity and understanding. Yin requires being still with oneself and reflecting on the truth of things. One cannot be in motion and in a state of reflection at the same time.

In a manner of speaking, Ben suffers from an imbalance of too much yang and underdeveloped yin. He is too busy trying to be on top, impressing others, achieving, and being important to reflect on the impact he has on other people. He suffers from a lack of awareness as well as a lack of appreciation about how to function within a team. Simply put, he does not place much value on being part of the team, despite the fact that the team can help ensure the success for which he strives.

So if you think you might have some Overstuffed PITA tendencies yourself, how can you become less overstuffed and more successful? Following are some approaches and strategies.

Be Patient with Your Own Needs and Desires to Be the Best

Humans need and want to achieve mastery over work situations in order to feel competent and capable as contributing members in the workplace. A sense of industry is a powerful human need and a glorious expression of people's individual interests and talents. The manual dexterity and exacting nature of a good carpenter are as much to be admired as the verbal ability and powers of persuasion exhibited by a popular politician.

Regardless of our chosen job or profession, it is a common desire to want to feel some degree of control, to believe we have a positive impact on outcomes in our place of work, and to feel appreciated for our unique contributions to the goals of the job. It also feels particularly good to get special recognition for a job well done, to be perceived as really gifted in a specific skill set, or to be nominated or appointed as leader of a team. These types of occurrences in the workplace are bonuses.

The lesson to be learned is that being the best is a noble goal, but excellence in any craft requires patience and perseverance. There is a balance to be struck in wanting to excel versus wanting to excel at all costs. If you pursue your goals with dedication, commitment, and character, the success will come in time. This pursuit does not require that you constantly overshadow others or be overstuffed to make it happen.

Replace Your Need for External Praise with Internal Pats on the Back

Unfortunately, the undeniable reality about work is that we don't typically get reinforced on a consistent basis with praise, rewards, accolades, or even words of encouragement. The result of this inconsistent schedule of rewards is that in those times of no pay-off, when you're getting no extra money, status, or emotional recognition, you have to generate the payoffs internally. You have to develop internal mechanisms that let you know that you are doing an okay job, that you possess unique and special skills, and that you do not necessarily lose when someone else wins.

Most of us go about the tasks of our day without our manager/supervisor stopping by our office to tell us how valuable we are or how much we contribute to our organizations. Whether or not we are aware of it, most of the time we satisfy ourselves by committing to a meaningful task and taking pride in doing a good job. Whether it's making a sale, designing a brochure, leading a team on a project, or developing a new marketing idea, we give ourselves "internal pats on the back" whenever we acknowledge that we played a role in a job well done.

Acknowledge the Value in Others

The key to not becoming an Overstuffed PITA is to be able to develop a self-generated ability to not have to be the top dog all the time in order to feel okay. If you find yourself headed down that path, work to prevent yourself from becoming toxically self-absorbed. It requires knowing that many people are multiskilled, capable, and useful and that this does not reduce the skills, capabilities, and utility of another. As a matter of fact, truly avoiding becoming an Overstuffed PITA means regularly putting other coworkers, team members, and subordinates ahead of yourself and giving credit to the group before seeking personal recognition.

Remember That You're Not in This Alone

Build your awareness of how you impact others on your team, in your unit, or in your workplace. Think of yourself as a part of a system of personalities that need to blend together in order to achieve a mission. Get feedback from a trusted colleague if you feel as though you cannot accurately access your interpersonal style and your character traits.

In an ideal world, your supervisor should point out these important features in end-of-the-year personnel evaluations. We realize, though, that this does not always happen, for a whole host of reasons. Therefore, it's up to you to seek out honest feedback on a regular basis from that trusted person who knows your work and has the courage to give it to you straight. Your job is to listen to the feedback, stew on it, digest it, and determine whether or not it rings true. Ultimately, your goal is to develop your ability to welcome this feedback, as hard as it might be to hear.

CHAPTER 5

The Soggy PITA: A Needy Whiner

Who in the world likes to eat a soggy pita? Whether the sogginess is the result of the dressing or the melted cheese, a pita that turns soggy is just so darn annoying to eat. You try patching the holes with your fingers or a napkin, but the soggy insides of the pita somehow make their way through. You might try folding the pita, using the nonsoggy parts to help stabilize the soggy parts, but that doesn't work either. It's now too big to put in your mouth. You usually end up "throwing in the towel" and asking for a knife and fork, converting your pita sandwich into a pita salad of sorts.

As annoying as it is to eat a soggy pita, it's much more annoying to work with one. You know who I'm talking about—the ones who are constantly whining about things: "I don't feel as though people appreciate all the hard work I've done on this project.... There's just way too much on my plate.... This week is really dragging.... Is it Friday yet?" Do any of these ring a bell? Soggy PITAs are also very needy, or high-maintenance. They need a lot of help working through issues or problems and frequently seek your "two cents" to make sure they're on the right track. Soggy PITAs need to *process* or talk through every negative interaction they had with a coworker or boss with everybody *except* the person they had the conflict with.

A Working Definition for the Soggy PITA

A Soggy PITA is a coworker who tends to be whiny, high-maintenance, needy, and afraid of addressing issues head on. Throughout this chapter, we refer to the people who display these characteristics as being "soggy." We also refer to those situations that tend to cause soggy behavior as "soggy situations."

The Soggy PITA at Work

While you'll see Soggy PITAs in a wide variety of settings, they tend to be the most soggy in everyday work situations, just hanging out around the office. The following scenario takes place in an office suite of 20 professionals working for a financial investment company. Sam has worked for 10 years as a financial planner. Lately, he has become increasingly unhappy at work.

A couple weeks ago, Sam got passed over for a promotion to become a financial manager. He felt that he had worked hard for the company and deserved the promotion. Someone who joined the firm only a few years ago was promoted over Sam. Understandably, Sam was greatly disappointed. Adding to his disappointment, Sam recently had a confrontation with Abby, a fellow financial planner, about his lack of follow-through with his work commitments.

Sam had offered to stay a half-hour late each day in case a customer needed to talk to a financial advisor during evening hours. However, over the past few weeks, Sam has been leaving a few minutes earlier for various reasons, often referring to important personal engagements. At the last staff meeting, Abby brought up a concern regarding Sam's coverage at the end of the day. Sam was upset with Abby for embarrassing him in front of his colleagues.

Famous Soggy PITAs

Here are some characters from popular television shows and movies who exemplify Soggy PITA characteristics:

- Jason Alexander as George Costanza (Seinfeld)
- David Schwimmer as Ross Geller (Friends)
- Ben Stiller as Gaylord "Greg" Focker (Meet the Parents)
- Charlie Brown (Peanuts)
- Bob Newhart as Dr. Robert "Bob" Hartley (The Bob Newhart Show)
- Eve Plumb as Jan Brady (The Brady Bunch)
- Brad Garrett as Robert Barone (Everybody Loves Raymond)
- Calista Flockhart as Ally McBeal (Ally McBeal)
- Eric McCormack as Will Truman (Will & Grace)
- Alan Ruck as Cameron Frye (Ferris Bueller's Day Off)
- Zach Braff as Dr. John "J. D." Dorian (Scrubs)

Sam's overall mood and demeanor have become more and more soggy at work. He's disgruntled over not being appreciated and respected enough to be considered for the financial manager position. In fact, Sam has been passed over on other occasions, so he has a long string of workplace disappointments. Over the past year, not a day went by that Sam didn't seek support and reassurance from his three trusted colleagues—Ted, Carey, and Nancy. Each of these colleagues deals with Sam's sogginess in his or her own way:

- Ted tends to be a bit "two-faced," telling Sam what Abby has been saying about his poor performance and, in turn, clueing Abby in on Sam's concerns.

- Carey is extremely nurturing and finds herself counseling and advising Sam.

- Nancy, on the other hand, tries to stay neutral. Although she cares about Sam as a colleague, she feels uncomfortable getting too immersed in his issues.

Here's a snapshot of a day in Sam's life at work. Sam came into work especially "down in the dumps" this day. Carey noticed this and stuck her head in Sam's office.

"Are you doing okay? You seem a little upset," Carey said. Sam asked if she had a minute, so Carey came into his office and closed the door behind her. After Carey pulled up a chair to Sam's desk, he shared his concerns in a self-pitying tone:

> *I just don't know what to do anymore. It seems like anything I try to do, nobody notices. I've been here for 10 years now, working my butt off, and this young whippersnapper gets the job that I deserved. I'm getting sick of being passed over.*

> *And then there's Abby...I think she's out to get me. I bet you she had something to do with me not getting promoted! She was talking to Ted about me the other day, saying that I don't have the same level of commitment to our company as I used to. I just can't win! You think I should have gotten the job, right? Don't you think that I have what it takes?*

With great concern, Carey replied, "That must be so frustrating…feeling like people are not appreciating you." This prompted Sam to continue venting for another 20 minutes, going on and on about his same old feelings of being misunderstood and underappreciated.

Later that afternoon, Abby approached Sam, saying that he needed to do a better job of taking care of his evening obligation. After Abby left, Sam went over to Nancy's office and asked whether she had a minute to talk. Nancy hesitated, but then said that she had a luncheon, but could talk for a few minutes. (Lately, Nancy had been trying to avoid Sam. It was becoming too much for her to handle emotionally because the conversations never seemed to lead to any type of resolution.) After hearing the (long) story from Sam regarding the dilemma he was in, Nancy tried to respond in a way that would keep this episode as short as possible:

> *Well, Sam, maybe you could check in with Abby to find out what exactly her issues are with you. Maybe she didn't have anything to do with your not being promoted. The only way you'll find out for sure is to ask her directly. On a different note, I wanted to let you know that I finished the report for the client that we were consulting about earlier in the week. Here, let me print you a copy.*

Once Sam received the printed report, he thanked Nancy and headed back to his office.

Near the end of the day, Sam ran into Ted in the hallway. Ted asked how things were going between him and Abby. After Sam gave a detailed explanation of his frustrations with Abby (repeating what he'd already shared with Ted two previous times), Ted informed him of a "recent development":

I talked to Abby this morning. She said that she thinks we should identify somebody else to stay after work because our evening clients aren't being handled appropriately. I reassured her that you have everything under control, but...

This "recent development" regarding evening-hour coverage that Ted so willingly shared caused additional concern for Sam. He spent the next 15 minutes huffing and complaining, and Ted affirmed his feelings of frustration.

Understanding the Soggy PITA

When you're dealing with a Soggy PITA, one of the most important things to realize is that, for whatever reason, your soggy coworker needs an extra dose of support and reassurance. Your coworker might be soggy due to his or her current troubling situation, previous disappointments, or a little bit of both. It's possible that your soggy coworker is seeking the emotional support that may be absent from his or her personal life. Or perhaps your coworker has multiple stressors in his or her life (for example, family issues or relationship problems) and very little support on the side. The sogginess could have developed from a whole host of reasons, but it's clear that your coworker's needs for support are not being met.

On the other hand, your coworker might have a highly sensitive temperament. In fact, there is the possibility that he or she receives lots of support from friends and family members, yet still brings personal needs into the workplace. It could even be that the Soggy PITA has gotten into the habit of whining and venting as a way to cope more effectively with his or her anxieties and concerns, and therefore experiences some sense of relief. At some point, you have to acknowledge and accept that some coworkers need a high level of encouragement and feedback.

No matter what the reason is, soggy coworkers tend to come across as more sensitive, dependent, and needy than the average person. The Soggy PITA has a greater need to talk things through and seek out others' approval. When addressing conflicts, such as the case of Sam and Abby, they tend to go around it instead of facing it head on.

As for all PITA types, there are varying degrees and frequencies of Soggy PITAs. Some coworkers are soggy all the time, no matter how positive their work environment and home life are. Some are soggy only when conflict occurs, whereas others become soggy when they're not feeling well. Obviously, working with the everyday Soggy PITA is a bigger challenge. It's easier to be supportive to a situational Soggy PITA because you can see the light at the end of the tunnel. Before thinking about how to cope with a Soggy PITA, determine how frequent and problematic the sogginess is.

Strategies for Coping with a Soggy PITA

Now that you understand the Soggy PITAs a little better, you're in a better position to cope more effectively as you encounter them in the workplace. Following are several strategies for coping more effectively with Soggy PITAs.

Have Some Compassion

In the spirit of wanting to develop and maintain positive working relationships, try to empathize with your soggy coworkers. Sometimes this is easier said than done. When you have five tasks to complete by the end of the day and it's already 3:30 in the afternoon, it's hard to feel compassion for a Soggy PITA who needs a few minutes of your time. Another reason it's difficult to empathize with soggy coworkers is that we all have our own stuff to deal with. So when a Soggy PITA goes on and on about an ongoing problem, like being the only one who has problems, it takes patience and generosity to lend an ear. Even though it's a challenge, try your best to empathize with your soggy coworkers.

Set Boundaries

Empathizing with your soggy coworkers doesn't mean that it's your responsibility to go to great lengths to make things better for them. You have a job to do, and unless you're the staff psychologist, your job isn't to provide counseling for your coworkers. It's important that you find ways to set boundaries and limit the amount of time you spend helping out the Soggy PITAs.

In our scenario, Carey essentially took on the role of counselor for Sam, showing a lot of compassion and concern for him. Carey reflected back his feelings by saying, "That must be difficult for you...." This is a response people often use to show empathy and to prompt a person to keep talking. This kind of approach invites Soggy PITAs to continue talking about their current "crisis" and to go back to such a caring coworker the next time they need somebody to lean on. Be realistic regarding how much time you can give soggy coworkers. Set your boundaries accordingly by finding ways to keep your interactions to a minimum.

Create an Exit Strategy

It's helpful to find appropriate ways to escape interactions with Soggy PITAs. The emphasis here is on the word "appropriate." Anybody can escape soggy coworkers by being rude and uncaring.

Simply saying "Good luck with that" and walking away can be an effective exit strategy. If you really want to cut the string on your working relationship with Soggy PITAs, that would be the way to go. But because we don't believe in being dismissive, and because you'll be forced to work with Soggy PITAs on projects from time to time, it's healthy to consider exit strategies that aren't so cold and abrupt.

If you recall from the scenario, Nancy used "diversion" as an exit strategy. After offering a possible solution to Sam's work dilemma, she diverted or derailed the situation by switching gears to a different work-related issue (printing out a report to share with Sam). In addition to the diversion strategy, here are a few other exit strategies to consider:

- **Postpone the interaction:** Once you hear the gist of your soggy coworker's issue and determine that it's not too severe, you can politely ask to continue the conversation at a later time. You might acknowledge his or her issue, but then inform your coworker that you have a project deadline or that you're currently swamped, and ask if you could try to catch up later in the day. Many times these issues tend to work themselves out thanks to one of the greatest healers: time.

- **Set limits up front:** As an alternative to postponing the conversation completely, you can agree to engage for a short while, letting your soggy coworker know how long you can give him or her. This might seem a bit rough, but there are ways of framing your time limit while still showing that you want to help. For example, upon being asked whether you have a minute to talk, you could reply, "Sam, I really need to get this report finished this morning, but I want to hear what's going on, so grab a seat and let's chat for a few minutes." Setting this limit right away puts you in a good position to stop the conversation at an appropriate time and remind your soggy coworker about your time crunch.

- **Redirect your soggy coworker:** When your soggy coworker's concern has to do with one of your other coworkers, you might feel uncomfortable or believe that it's inappropriate to participate in the conversation. Encourage your soggy coworker to address his or her concern directly with the other coworker. You might want to express that you respect them both, and that you feel a little awkward getting in the middle of the situation. You might also want to provide some assurance that, if your soggy coworker addresses the issue respectfully, the other coworker will most likely be receptive and willing to work things out.

When Your Direct Report Is a Soggy PITA: Tips for Managers

- Establish a trusting, caring relationship with your soggy employees early. You'll build more loyalty with your soggy employees and get more productivity from them if you are more supportive and nurturing. It's the quickest way to a soggy employee's heart. Plus, establishing trust will enable you to experience more success when you need to address difficult issues concerning a soggy employee's performance.

- Don't allow soggy employees to eat up other coworkers' time. Although it's difficult to do, you must confront your soggy employees when you've determined that their soggy behaviors and interactions are taking too much time and energy away from their coworkers. It's difficult for many people to find a tactful way to tell soggy coworkers that they're wasting their time at work, and quite frankly, it's not their job to do so. Furthermore, people usually don't like to go to a soggy coworker's boss (you) and complain. During the rare times when coworkers complain to you about your soggy employee, however, you can encourage them to set limits and utilize exit strategies (described earlier in this chapter).

- Help your soggy employees become less soggy. Once you've exposed the soggy behavior and discussed its associated costs, help your soggy direct reports develop strategies for becoming less soggy (see "Strategies for Becoming Less Soggy" near the end of this chapter). This is a great way to offer support to your soggy employees.

Realize that every work relationship is unique because it consists of two unique people. So when you're deciding among exit strategies, it's also important to consider the following:

- Your comfort level

- The degree of sogginess the coworker demonstrates

- The severity of the situation

In the end, it helps to be proactive in identifying appropriate exit strategies ahead of time so that you're ready to employ them during the next soggy interaction you have.

Don't Make Things Worse: Stay Somewhat Neutral

There are two ways you can make things worse when dealing with soggy coworkers. First, you can increase the sogginess in coworkers by excessively putting yourself in the counselor role like Carey did in the scenario. Now and again, we all find ourselves taking on the counselor role, particularly for those coworkers we care about, but it's important that we don't do it too much. We already showed how that can perpetuate the situation.

Second, you can intensify the degree of sogginess by adding fuel to the fire. In the scenario, Ted fueled Sam's fire by sharing additional information from Abby, the coworker who had the conflict with Sam. It's important to be neutral to a certain extent. Although Carey stuck her nose too far into the soggy situation (and spent too much of her work time), at least she helped Sam by giving him a lot of emotional support. Plus, Carey didn't make the situation any worse. On the other hand, Ted stuck his nose too far in and helped *nobody* while perpetuating the negative situation. We think it's clear: Nancy handled the soggy situation the best out of the three, whereas Ted handled it most poorly.

Confront Soggy Colleagues When Necessary

As you've seen with other PITAs, you sometimes need to confront soggy colleagues head-on if nothing else works. The hope is that if you do what Nancy did—staying neutral and employing exit strategies—your soggy coworkers will get a clue and limit their soggy interactions. When that doesn't happen, you'll need to find a tactful way to confront your coworkers.

Just as there's no right exit strategy for everybody, there's not one approach to confronting Soggy PITAs that's best for all. Think about an approach that you're comfortable with and that won't hurt the working relationship. It's hard to do this without the confrontation "stinging" your coworker a little bit. If it doesn't sting, you're probably not getting through and the soggy behavior will likely continue. So you have to be okay with the fact that what you say might not be pleasant for your coworker to hear.

Let's play out the scenario a bit more, assuming that Sam didn't get the message from Nancy when she tried to derail him. Here's one way that Nancy could have confronted Sam without doing too much damage:

> *Sam, can I talk to you about something? I know you've been down lately. I've been feeling bad lately that I haven't been able to help you out more, but as you know, I've been asked to take on some difficult clients and am taking classes at night, and I'm spread too thin. Lately, I've been taking work home with me almost every night, and it's not fair to my family. I just wanted to talk to you about this so you understand times when I'm not able to lend an ear; I value our working relationship and don't want you to ever think that I don't care.*

Again, this is just one approach. You will need to alter this approach to fit your style, comfort level, and circumstances. Most importantly, because there are feelings at stake (and the hypersensitivity of a soggy coworker), be sure to spend enough time critically thinking about your approach before you use it.

Appreciate What the Soggy PITA Brings to the Table

To help you get through some of the challenges that come from working with soggy people, remember the good qualities that usually reside within Soggy PITAs. Soggy PITAs are usually sensitive and considerate of others' feelings. The hypersensitivity that exists in many soggy coworkers, when channeled effectively, can be helpful when working with customers or coworkers who are in conflict or crisis. Because Soggy PITAs know what it feels like to be down and go through difficult situations, they tend to show empathy toward others in need.

Professionals Increasing Their Awareness: Strategies for Becoming Less Soggy

As highlighted in chapter 1, everybody has the potential to be a PITA from time to time. Aren't there times when you're feeling a little down and need some support? Haven't you ever complained about being too busy? You can easily fall into the soggy trap, especially when colleagues like Carey make it easy for you. As always, the key to keeping your sogginess in check is to increase your awareness of your own soggy tendencies. Following are strategies for increasing your self-awareness and keeping your Soggy PITA tendencies in check.

Determine When You Are Most Likely to Be Soggy

A good place to start is to put your finger on those work situations or times when you become soggy. Do you tend to take your personal problems to work? Are you a little soggy due to being back at work after a big, fun-packed weekend? Are you quick to complain about how busy you are? Do you avoid confrontation and talk about difficult coworkers to other, more trusted coworkers? Think back to those times when you've been soggy and try to identify those situations that tend to bring out your sogginess.

Examine and Challenge Your Sogginess

Now that you've pinpointed times at work when your sogginess tends to show up, ask yourself why you are soggy during those times. Is your behavior justified? You also need to determine which soggy behavior is no big deal, and which affects coworkers and needs to be altered. For example, venting to a trusted colleague once in a while when your plate is extra-full can be therapeutic for you and not a big deal to your colleague. On the other hand, sticking your head into the office of a colleague four times a day to complain about your job can have a negative effect on his or her morale and take too much of your coworker's time.

Your soggy behavior, however, is more likely to adversely affect *you* and your reputation. Pitying yourself too frequently in front of colleagues, for example, will cause your colleagues to want to avoid you and to lose respect for you as a professional.

Create a New Recipe for Firming Up Your Soggy Behavior

Now that you're more aware of when you become soggy and you've identified those soggy situations that are most problematic, think creatively of ways to firm up some of the sogginess. For many people, the soggy behavior is just a habit that formed over the years. If Sam, for example, had increased his awareness of his soggy habit of sharing too many of his problems with colleagues, he could have made a decision to seek out a trusted friend or professional counselor to help him through his recent disappointment. This would be a much better approach to help improve relationships at work.

Face Your Fear of Confrontation

Confrontation is difficult for everybody, but for Soggy PITAs, it can feel particularly unpleasant to engage in and persevere through conflict. Here are some steps to help you deal more effectively with confrontation:

1. **Own the fact that tactful confrontation is *good*.**
    Sometimes doing nothing is worse than doing something. This is usually the case when dealing with confrontation. One of the worst things you can do for a working relationship is to let negative thoughts and feelings you have toward a coworker fester up inside you. Out of respect for your coworker and the morale of your unit or department, you must find a way to confront him or her. None of us likes to hear that we're being talked about behind our back. Tactfully confronting coworkers in times of conflict is the right thing to do.

2. **Find the right time and place to confront.** Once you realize that you must approach your coworker, determine the best time and place to confront him or her. If your coworker is having an especially bad day or week, you might want to postpone the confrontation. As for the place, it's very rare that confronting a coworker in public or in front of other coworkers is the best place. Consider initiating a meeting in your office to confront your coworker behind closed doors.

3. **Confront tactfully yet firmly.** Think of an approach that won't put your colleague on the defensive. Own parts of the conflict that you could improve on, and start with that. Then choose your words wisely regarding the parts that you're asking your coworker to adjust. But make sure

that you stand your ground. If you tend to be a bit soggy during these trying times, it's natural to give in too quickly. If you can't come to a healthy compromise, it's better to agree to disagree than to lose ground.

Have Your "Soggy Antenna" Up at All Times

As you read in previous chapters, you need to keep your antenna up at all times to detect signals of your own sogginess coming on. You can break soggy habits only if you're aware of them when they're occurring. Throughout the day, people do things without thinking much about them. Signals that your antenna might pick up are fear, vulnerability, intimidation, or insecurity.

Early on, you'll most likely need to manually put up your antenna during those soggy work situations you identified. Eventually, your soggy antenna will go up automatically as you transform your soggy habits. In the scenario, Sam could have used a soggy antenna to keep him from bothering so many of his coworkers.

Answer the "How Ya Doing?" Question with the Glass Half-Full

With all the pressures and responsibilities at work, it's common to talk soggy when asked how you're doing. The most typical response to the question "How are things at work?" is "Busy!" Well, guess what? We're all busy! Don't you get tired of hearing how busy your colleagues say they are? One concrete way to at least appear less soggy is to stop telling everybody how busy you are. Instead of complaining about *how* busy you are, you could focus more on *what* it is that's keeping you so busy. Here's a sample response to the question, "How are things at work?"

Things have been pretty busy. The Burns account has been keeping me hopping. However, it's been interesting to work with a client that has as many divisions as Burns has. How are things for you?

Notice the balance. The respondent could be honest about how busy he was, but also talk about how interesting the work has been. There are plenty of people complaining about things at work; go against the grain and focus more on the positive.

CHAPTER 6

The Sloppy PITA:
Disorganized and Oblivious

The gyro, the original pita sandwich of Greek origin, is completely delicious but consists of a highly messy concoction of lamb, tomato, and cucumber sauce that almost always ends up running down your arm. No matter how well intended you are to hold it together in the beginning, the gyro always wins and you end up cursing and reaching for the napkins.

You probably have a PITA in your life whose sloppiness is causing you problems. In contrast to the Overstuffed PITA, the Sloppy PITA is much less toxic in that this type of person does not generate nearly as much anger and resentment among his or her peers. Often, people of this particular style are likeable, friendly, engaging, and warm. The fact that the sloppy types ultimately become a pain in the ass has less to do with any oppressive or self-serving personality traits than with the fact that they are oblivious to detail and structure and their impact on other people's work lives. If sloppy people could exist in a vacuum and the remainder of the workplace could operate around them, they might not be PITAs at all. However, their style of not following workplace structures, of being disorganized, of not attending to detail, and of not thinking through their tasks in any logical way makes them a real nuisance to the people picking up the pieces.

The unsystematic way that many Sloppy PITAs conduct their work lives can also flow into their communication style, which can be aimless and excessive. Their audience often fidgets in their seats wondering when the point will be made and the period will appear to finish the monologue. To the credit of the Sloppy PITA, it's not like the information being presented is unimportant. In fact, the information might be completely necessary and highly useful; however, it is packaged in such a way that you are forced to sift through the barrage of words to find the meat in the message (or the lamb in the cucumber sauce).

Sloppy PITAs exist in practically everyone's workplace, yet chances are that they are not your administrative assistants, your bankers, or your accountants because these positions require a high degree of organization and attention to detail. This is not to say that there are not many Sloppy PITAs in positions of importance. They are often able to pull off high-level jobs because they can be people with ideas and motivation who can juggle many tasks. Yet you can bet their success hinges on the existence of top-notch administrative assistants to help them keep it all together.

A Working Definition for the Sloppy PITA

A Sloppy PITA is a coworker who tends to be disorganized, inattentive to detail, imprecise in work tasks, and generally "all over the place." Throughout this chapter, we refer to the people who display these characteristics as being "sloppy." We also refer to those situations that tend to cause sloppy behaviors as "sloppy situations."

The Sloppy PITA at Work

Consider this example of a Sloppy PITA in academia. Dr. Sidney Slack is a professor at a liberal arts college where she teaches English and creative writing. She has taught at the same institution for 20 years and she is a well-known figure within the English department. Dr. Slack is a talented writer and scholar who has published numerous articles and books in her specialty area. She is a woman with a wealth of knowledge. Being in her presence for any significant period of time reveals that she is passionate about literature and the written word.

As a lecturer, Dr. Slack is animated and charismatic. Students take her class just to experience her energetic outbursts and her frequent tangents, which are lively and engaging, if not completely on the subject. Her lectures are 50 percent inspiration and 50 percent free association. It's a crap shoot to predict where one of her lectures might lead and whether it will be remotely related to either creative writing or English literature.

Dr. Slack routinely neglects to hand back papers in a reasonable amount of time, which annoys her students and regularly appears on her end-of-semester teaching evaluations. Student evaluations indicate that they appreciate her for her energy and her ability to entertain; however, her total scores are countered by her inability to stick to a syllabus and her trouble with staying on task. Students who need a high degree of structure and organization are particularly put off by Dr. Slack's style. She also has problems with getting student grades in on time for end-of-semester reporting, which has gotten her into hot water with the dean and with parents of her students.

Within her department, Dr. Slack's brilliance as a scholar is widely acknowledged. But she is perceived as hampered by her lack of organization, her inability to implement any structure into her teaching, and her lack of awareness about the impact that these deficits have on the people around her. Dr. Slack also has a spotty record for attending departmental faculty meetings. When she is present, she moseys into the meetings 10 to 15 minutes late, often apologetic and humorously poking fun at herself.

In terms of the departmental hierarchy, Dr. Slack has not been the popular choice for departmental chair, despite the fact that she is an accomplished senior faculty member. Although Dr. Slack is respected and even well liked by her colleagues, they cannot bring themselves to appoint her chair of the department out of fear of the administrative loose ends and oversights that might ensue, even with the assistance of a solid administrative assistant (and where might they find such a martyr, anyway?). The fact that she has not been appointed departmental chair has been a sore topic for Dr. Slack, who believes that she has earned the title and the recognition after all her years of service.

Famous Sloppy PITAs

Here are some characters from popular television shows and movies who exemplify Sloppy PITA characteristics:

- Walter Matthau/Jack Klugman as Oscar Madison (*The Odd Couple*)

- McLean Stevenson as Lt. Colonel Henry Braymore Blake (*M*A*S*H*)

- Ally Sheedy as Allison Reynolds (*The Breakfast Club*)

- George Wendt as Norm Peterson *(Cheers)*

- Tom Cruise as Lt. Daniel Kaffee *(A Few Good Men)*

- Owen Wilson as Randolph Dupree *(You, Me and Dupree)*

- Casey Kasem as Norville "Shaggy" Rogers *(Scooby Doo)*

- Kevin James as Doug Heffernan *(The King of Queens)*

- Christopher Lloyd as Reverend Jim Ignatowski *(Taxi)*

- John Candy as Del Griffith *(Planes, Trains and Automobiles)*

In terms of compensation, Dr. Slack has received the same annual pay increases as her peers, an issue which might seem unfair, but is unfortunately common in the faculty ranks of higher education. Thus far, the dean of the college, Terry Tight, has been the one to provide feedback to Dr. Slack about her work performance. But Dr. Slack has not taken the feedback seriously because there are no real penalties for being an average performer. Also, she uses a number of rationalizations to prevent the feedback from sinking in.

The following exchange between Dean Tight and Dr. Slack demonstrates Dr. Slack's casual response to the dean's efforts at providing some corrective feedback.

Dean Tight: You know, Dr. Slack, this is really hard for me to bring up, but I thought you deserved some feedback about why you have not been recommended to be department chair. From what I'm hearing from colleagues and what your student evaluations are indicating, it seems like you have a problem with organizing yourself.

Dr. Slack: (Chuckles) That damn organization stuff again.

Dean Tight: Yeah, you know how it is. I'm aware that there's a lot of flexibility in this profession for being more "casual," but the faculty really need someone who can stay on top of things. More importantly, the students are creating a little bit of fuss about not getting papers back on time and your not sticking to the syllabus.

Dr. Slack: Come on, Dean Tight, that's not why you hired me. You hired me for my ideas and my love of teaching, not for being an office manager. You get from me what you really need, someone to fire up the classroom. I find it hard to believe that students, and you guys, can't get beyond this organizational stuff and see what's really important. After all, I got tenured because I teach and write well, not because I can balance my checkbook.

Because she is tenured faculty, Dr. Slack is aware that she will not lose her job for "something as trivial as being poorly organized." "Plus, who really wants to do all the departmental grunt work, anyway?" she thinks, a rationalization that infuriates her more dutiful colleagues.

Okay, so it appears as though we are dealing with the stereotypical absent-minded professor, right? What's the big deal, you ask? Aside from the fact that Dr. Slack's organizational problems adversely impact her students' learning experience, she also experiences some adversity as the result of her unwillingness to look at her Sloppy PITA tendencies. Dr. Slack is more sensitive than she lets on about her colleagues' annoyance with her. She is hurt by the fact that people take jabs at her for being forgetful, for being "out there," and for being irresponsible. She also feels unappreciated and confused because she is a hard worker and she takes her subject and her teaching seriously. Although she doesn't often show it, Dr. Slack is frustrated by the way things have evolved in her department and for being labeled "the Sloppy PITA."

Understanding the Sloppy PITA

Although the Sloppy PITA's deficits are probably reflective of his or her personality type, these behaviors and ways of relating to people are much less offensive and disturbing than other PITA types, such as the Overstuffed PITA. There could be a number of reasons for the Sloppy PITA's organizational deficits, inattention to detail, or disregard for structure. Perhaps this person has some form of inattentive ADHD, a biologically based deficit, or a deeply ingrained style. But it's not our role as supervisors or colleagues to be the Sloppy PITA's psychological diagnostician. It is our role, however, to develop a general functional mindset about Sloppy PITAs in order to make our own adjustments for coping with the style.

In Dr. Slack's case, she has fortunately chosen a profession that has accommodated her Sloppy PITA characteristics. In many ways this shows how insightful Dr. Slack is, in that she was either consciously or unconsciously aware of the fact that she would not function well in a highly structured occupation such as office manager or accountant. Her propensity for teaching and verbally free-associating is common to people who are energized by concepts and theories and making linkages between their rush of ideas. It's much like playing dot-to-dot with concepts where she is the only one who can see the whole picture.

Many Sloppy PITAs' ways of thinking and organizing their world are generally different because of their hardwiring and their makeup. Although they might try to make genuine efforts at greater degrees of organization, this will never really become one of their strengths. Most neuropsychologists recognize that brain anatomy and functioning heavily impact people who are chronically disorganized, late, or incapable of managing detail. In the same way that great athletes have incredible genetically based hand-eye coordination while other people struggle to dribble a ball, some people are on top of every detail and others just can't seem to pull it together.

Acknowledging the potential neurological basis of Sloppy PITA behavior should give you some degree of acceptance and empathy about their organizational struggles and enable you to cope with them better. Again, it's not so much that these people face challenges and deficits that make them PITAs. It's more about their unwillingness to acknowledge a problem or area of weakness and blindly continuing to engage in behaviors without any awareness, recognition, or effort to improve in specific areas.

Strategies for Coping with a Sloppy PITA

Understanding that biological hardwiring is most likely at the root of Sloppy PITA thought processes and behavior, you can approach your PITA with a spirit of empathy and understanding rather than blame, irritation, or hostility.

However, we do have to acknowledge that extreme disorganized behavior, lack of attention to detail, or chronic lateness, as well as a host of other sloppy habits, make other people's lives unnecessarily difficult. Depending on how bad the situation is, it's not okay if Dr. Slack cannot stick to topic in her lectures, cannot remotely follow a syllabus, or rarely if ever gets her homework assignments and tests graded and returned on time. The challenge is to make Dr. Slack aware of her behaviors, to get her to own that a problem does exist, and to let her know that she has to work to get better in certain organizational areas in order to improve her workplace performance.

As with any of the PITA behaviors mentioned in the preceding chapters, the goal is not to scold, approach angrily, degrade, or ridicule the person you are trying to impact. Also, keep in mind that the best approaches differ based on the power relationship that you might have with the Sloppy PITA in your work life. In the case of Dr. Slack, obviously, it would be easier for a supervisor to approach her rather than a colleague or a student. Dr. Slack's students might have to take more subtle approaches, such as making specific requests to get papers back sooner or to review material that was inadequately covered the first time in class. These kinds of specific requests are much easier to make than requesting changes in the PITA's organizational style or a more general focus on managing time or detail.

The same philosophy holds true for the Sloppy PITA in your own workplace. The hardest part is getting the person to be open to the problem, to lower his or her defensiveness, and to buy into the creation of potential solutions. Once the PITA buys in, you can then partner with him or her to generate ideas that can lead to more organized behaviors. In contrast to the Overstuffed PITA, who has to become aware of vague psychological and behavioral tendencies in work relationships, the Sloppy PITA has the advantage of being able to focus on specific, concrete work functions.

We suggest the following approaches for coping with a Sloppy PITA. These recommendations are a combination of eliciting change on the part of the PITA and changing your own approach when working with a Sloppy PITA.

Don't Assume Intentional Sloppiness

Don't assume that Sloppy PITAs are as aware of the problem as you are. Because their behavior is so much a part of the fabric of their being, and on some level their way of existing makes sense to them, they are not aware of the frustration that their behavior causes for people around them. If and when you approach your particular Sloppy PITAs, assume that they are not intentionally trying to make your work life miserable. They might actually be surprised to hear that their behaviors are causing problems for other people.

Know That the Sloppy PITA Is Not Necessarily a Sealed PITA

Sloppy PITAs are probably not nearly as resistant to feedback as other types of PITAs. Although Sloppy PITAs come in many forms and have many different personality features, the characteristic of being disorganized in thought and action does not necessarily make these people highly sensitive as well. Most often you can proceed with the same purpose as you would with any non-PITA employees, with the assumption that they want to perform better and that they care about the quality of their work.

When Your Direct Report Is a Sloppy PITA: Tips for Managers

- Don't confuse likeability with responsibility. The more casual, easygoing sloppy direct reports may be popular among staff, but you still need to hold them to task.

- Map out a clear game plan with sloppy direct reports. Broad and vague directives will not work. Be specific about the tasks and behaviors that need changing and methods for making the changes.

- Regular check-ins with Sloppy PITAs are the best way to ensure progress. Have them explain to you any practical methods they are using to shore up their organizational skills and attention to detail.

Be a Helpful Partner in Nonsloppy Solutions

Approach your Sloppy PITAs as a partner in finding a solution rather than as someone who is merely registering a complaint. In Dr. Slack's case, your approach as a supervisor might be to inform her that there has been some consistent feedback suggesting that she is not covering items in class that she puts on her syllabus. Doing this creates awareness of the problem. You might also follow up by engaging in a collaborative conversation about how she can structure her lectures to cover all her topics. This might result in Dr. Slack reducing the amount of information that she intends to cover in class or more diligently sticking to the syllabus and monitoring her tendency to go off track.

This collaborative approach lets Dr. Slack know that you are an ally in helping her be successful rather than an adversary whose motive is to be critical. Regardless of the person or scenario, this problem-solving approach should work best with all Sloppy PITAs.

Appreciate Different Ways of Working

Demonstrate your acceptance and appreciation of different personality styles. Numerous personality tests and articles teach people to value equally the multiple ways of existing and working in the world. One lesson that continually emerges is that some styles are best suited to certain job functions. To put it simply, there are bean-counters and salesmen, those who plan the party and those who are the life of the party.

Although Sloppy PITAs might not follow the same rules of functioning as more planful, organized, step-by-step thinkers and doers, they might be excellent at perceiving whole concepts coming together, in addition to having big-picture vision. In some work tasks and with some workplace goals, conceptual, big-picture thinking might be the needed skill set for achieving the best results.

Use Practical Resources

Proven techniques can work well with Sloppy PITAs. There are lots of books and articles about time-management and self-management. Specific tried-and-true techniques (such as keeping daily planners, taking detailed notes, and writing outlines) can work well with Sloppy PITAs.

For supervisors who are trying to get these people to change some of their sloppy ways, practice with organization techniques can help to pull things together. In essence, you are helping them put structure into a naturally unstructured way of existing in the world.

Remember That a Subtle Approach Will Increase Chances of Buy-In

Be careful about coming on too strong with suggestions and corrections for Sloppy PITAs. Like all human beings, they will be sensitive and protective of the methods that have gotten them this far in life. Although there might be objectively better and more efficient means for functioning in the workplace, people are reluctant to change. Coming on too forcefully or too confident that your own method is right might not get you very far. Develop your own capability to offer feedback and alternative suggestions in sensitive ways that increase the likelihood of buy-in.

Be Aware of Your Own Needs to Do It Your Way

Notice your own needs to have control. Sometimes our own overdeveloped needs to have things neat and tidy and in their place can make us overly zealous when it comes to expecting order from others. Part of coping means to accurately and honestly examine our own issues and make self-adjustments accordingly. Ask yourself questions such as the following:

- How well do you tolerate ambiguity?

- Do you always need order and structure in your work setting?

- Does the situation always require such an emphasis on providing detail?

- Are you annoyed because you can't control Sloppy PITAs and because they do things differently, or do they really create disruptions and difficulties in the workplace?

Again, effective coping does not always mean changing the other person. Perhaps you need to look at your own reactions and how you can alter your thoughts and behaviors so that you don't respond in such negative ways.

Appreciate What the Sloppy PITA Brings to the Table

Mentioning positive qualities associated with being disorganized and all over the place might seem strange. But it's our experience that other desirable traits tend to go hand in hand with the sloppy style. In contrast to the Rigid PITA, Sloppy PITAs can be more relaxed, go-with-the-flow, and casual in their interactions. This can make them enjoyable coworkers who don't take everything so seriously. On your team, you might be thankful that there are some sloppies to balance out the rigids.

Professionals Increasing Their Awareness: Strategies for Becoming Less Sloppy

If you think you might be a Sloppy PITA, it's important to be more conscious and aware of where your disorganization or sloppiness creates the most problems for you. Then you can make a conscious and determined effort to intervene in some way. Many people are not sloppy across the board, but they might have one specific area where they need some help. Other people might see sloppy tendencies running through many aspects of their lives. For example, if you tend to lose track of the organization of your thoughts when you speak or make presentations, focus on making outlines ahead of time that help keep you on track. Another easy intervention is to practice making your presentation within a designated time limit so that you don't have the time or space to ramble.

The Sloppy PITA who develops self-awareness can achieve results much faster and much more directly than other types of PITAs who work to develop self-awareness. Why is this? Primarily, the reason is that self-awareness on the part of the Sloppy PITA can lead to very observable, concrete actions and goals that are easily measured. If, for example, Dr. Slack acknowledges that she does go off track with her lectures and that she really does need to make sure the proper material is covered, she can make concrete, practical changes that would help her to do so. Whatever her final interventions might be (for example, developing a more effective outline and devoting specific blocks of lecture time for each topic area), the potential for observable success is great.

Dr. Slack might find that a few concrete interventions help her to complete her lecture in the designated amount of time and that all the topics on the syllabus for that day get covered. Dr. Slack might even find that with improved self-awareness she could employ her graduate assistants or student helpers to remind her of how well she is sticking to topic and staying on task. The rewards for Dr. Slack's behavior change can be immediate and clear: She will not get behind with her material and students will reward her with positive feedback and evaluations.

Following are some approaches and strategies for becoming less sloppy.

Be Patient with Your Sloppy Tendencies

Being patient with yourself is important if you have Sloppy PITA tendencies. Being organized, structured, and attentive to detail does not come naturally to many people. Just like some people are beautiful singers, talented artists, and amazing athletes, others are spectacular organizers and managers of detail in the world. Thank heaven they exist to manage the detail for the rest of us. They make exceptional event planners, office managers, financial accountants and analysts, and practically any other thing that requires a high degree of planning and pulling things together. It is and they are a thing of beauty.

The ultimate lesson, however, lies in the fact that most of us do not possess this as a natural talent and we have to work at it. If you are in the process of working on your sloppy tendencies, congratulate yourself for making small strides toward pulling it together. Small successes definitely count as you work on changing sloppy behaviors. You should view as individual successes every meeting that you attend on time, every list that you make, and every outline you create.

Be Conscientious About Your Sloppy Impact

Care enough about the work you perform and about becoming a competent professional. If you care about what you do in your chosen occupational role, you will work to become better at areas where you might have sloppy tendencies. If Dr. Slack cared enough about her students' learning process and successes, she would take a serious look at her teaching style.

Detect Your Coworkers' Reactions and Comments

Pay attention to how other people in your work unit, team, class, or agency respond to your organizational style and attention to detail. If you have received questions or comments on more than one occasion such as

- "Could you get me that a little sooner next time?"

- "Could you make it on time today, the topic is important?" or

- "I'm having trouble following what you are saying,"

you should start paying attention to any sloppy tendencies and patterns that you might be exhibiting. Because colleagues are sensitive to your feelings, they might deliver this type of feedback in a humorous form, where they take a little jab or seem playful in their delivery. Make a point to notice comments such as these even if they are couched in humor. One or two comments might not constitute a problem. Multiple comments are probably signs of a pattern.

Notice Your Own Feelings

Pay attention to your own feelings regarding your organizational style and attention to detail. Ask yourself questions such as these:

- Do you get frustrated by not being able to find things on your desk?

- Do you find yourself embarrassed by being consistently late to meetings and having to apologize for not leaving enough time to walk, travel, or park?

- Do you find it difficult to deliver your thoughts in a well-organized or logical manner when making presentations or communicating your agenda?

These could all be signs that you have some Sloppy PITA behaviors that you might need to correct.

Consult with Your Nonsloppy Colleagues

If you suspect you are a Sloppy PITA, consult with a valued colleague, friend, supervisor, or anyone you trust. Talking with trusted colleagues is extremely important with all the PITA types because even the most self-aware people are not able to see themselves completely accurately. Although you might perceive bits of truth about your own behaviors, a valued other party can help you fill in the blanks. Allow the information to pass through your filter and don't be too quick to dismiss it. A good method is to observe and assess their feedback for a few days before you either discount it or accept it.

Adopt Best Practices

If you become aware that you have sloppy areas, consult well-organized people about their best methods for keeping things together. If you are observant, you will notice that the most organized and structured people in your life possess some tried-and-true methods for tackling complex tasks. Many of them have systems for writing notes, managing time, structuring their work days, answering e-mail, organizing their desktops (both physical and electronic), making presentations, remembering facts, studying, and even organizing thoughts in their heads. It's also important to remember that people like to be helpful and to offer their expertise, so don't be shy or ashamed of asking for advice. You may find out that at one time they struggled in the same areas that you do.

CHAPTER 7

The Make-Your-Own (Rigid) PITA:
Picky and Inflexible

I know you've been there. You're in line to order a "make-your-own" sandwich—a sub or a burger or, you guessed it, a pita. You haven't eaten for a while, so you just want to buy your pita and wolf it down. But the guy in line ahead of you is taking forever, mulling over every possible pita choice known to mankind. His indecision starts with the pita pocket itself: "Do you have a multigrain pita? Or how about a whole-wheat pita? Which one is fresher?" he asks. Then we move to the meat and cheese: "Do you have honey ham? Is it low-sodium? What kind of cheese do you have? Could I have the Swiss cheese lightly toasted so that only the edges are melted?" And finally, the fixings: "Just a touch of vinegar, and light on the mayo. I'd like a few sweet peppers—not too many—and I'd like some grilled onions…do you have red onions? And let's throw on a few tomatoes. Are they garden fresh? Do you have sundried tomatoes? As for spices, I'd like a pinch of salt and pepper, and a shake of oregano." All the while, you're thinking to yourself, "Come on, man, you're not buying a house here. Get a life!"

You're lucky if the only interaction you have with a picky, Rigid PITA is contained to a chance encounter in a sandwich joint. Many people are forced to work with Rigid PITAs on a daily basis. Rigid PITAs like to have things done their own way (hence the term "Make-Your-Own PITA") and have difficulty bending and compromising. They see the world in a certain way and can't understand why you don't see it that way, too. The Rigid PITA isn't the loudest, most vocal, in-your-face kind of PITA; the Rigid PITA just sort of gnaws away at you over time.

A Working Definition for the Make-Your-Own (Rigid) PITA

Because "Make-Your-Own PITA" is a mouthful (pun fully intended), we'll primarily refer to this person as a Rigid PITA. Our working definition of a Rigid PITA is a coworker who tends to be picky, particular, stubborn, rigid, inflexible, and uncompromising. Throughout this chapter, we refer to the people who display these characteristics as "Rigid PITAs."

The Rigid PITA at Work

This particular work scenario takes place in a human resources (HR) consulting firm. The HR firm is offering a benefits seminar to HR representatives in the region. The seminar provides an overview of different benefits packages that focus on various healthcare, insurance, retirement, and childcare benefit options.

The CEO of the HR consulting firm gave four employees the project of developing an informational brochure that would be given to the seminar participants. Rick (the featured Rigid PITA) was assigned to work with Rita, a Rigid PITA herself; Fred, a free-spirited, flexible coworker; and Hallie, a savvy, experienced professional.

During the first of several scheduled meetings, the four-member project team had two goals to reach by the end of the meeting: first, to determine the order in which the benefits would be listed in the brochure, and second, to establish an overall design format to use. There was a lot of conflict in trying to reach the first goal. Everybody except Rick thought that health care should be presented first. Rick felt strongly that retirement options should be presented first, and he wasn't going to go down without a fight: "We have to remember that a high number of the participants are over the age of 50, so retirement will be at the forefront of their minds. I think it would be a mistake to start off with health care on our brochure."

Famous Rigid PITAs

Here are some characters from popular television shows and movies who exemplify Rigid PITA characteristics:

- Courteney Cox as Monica Gellar *(Friends)*

- Jerry Seinfeld as Jerry Seinfeld *(Seinfeld)*

- Demi Moore as Lt. Cdr. JoAnne Galloway *(A Few Good Men)*

- Jack Lemmon / Tony Randall as Felix Ungar *(The Odd Couple)*

- David Hyde Pierce as Dr. Niles Crane *(Frasier)*

- Lucy Liu as Ling Woo *(Ally McBeal)*

- Cybill Shepherd as Madelyn "Maddie" Hayes *(Moonlighting)*

- Meg Ryan as Sally Albright *(When Harry Met Sally...)*

Rita wasn't going to budge from her position, either: "Well, I can't imagine a benefits brochure that doesn't put health care at the top of the list. I mean, one's health is the most important benefit, period! Without health, people have nothing."

Rick stood his ground by replying, "Well, sure, nobody denies that health care is a primary benefit. But it's important to tailor our brochure to the audience, and after talking to a few HR reps who will be attending, I think it's obvious that retirement options are most important to them at this point in time."

Fred (the flexible, easygoing member) was getting tired of this petty arguing and offered his opinion: "Does it really matter which one is listed first? I mean, as long as we're including both of them, who really cares? I say we flip a coin and get on with it."

Rita disagreed: "Well, I think it does matter; our company name will be all over this brochure, and we're making a statement that retirement is more important than health care if we list it first. We'll lose credibility with the HR reps if it looks like we don't recognize what's most important."

Rick just had to respond: "I really don't think we'll lose our credibility; I think that's a stretch. What I think we'll gain is some respect and a stronger connection, since we're hitting them with something that resonates with them. They'll be more inclined to read the whole brochure if we start the thing off with a bang."

Rita replied, "I think it's important to start things off right as well, but I don't think beginning with retirement options is the best way. You talked to only three people out of 50 or so who will attend the seminar. I'm sure if we polled all 50 we'd get a different result."

Hallie (the experienced, level-headed professional) finally offered her opinion: "You both have good points, but, like Fred, I don't think it's going to make or break the brochure. And since most of us are comfortable with health care being listed first, let's go with that for now. After we provide all the content and see what the whole brochure looks like, we can revisit it. Plus, we have only 15 minutes left to establish our overall design format."

The project team had similar challenges deciding on a design format. Rick wanted to use photos and Rita wanted graphics without pictures. Rick felt that the photos would help the topics come to life, but Rita thought using them would cost too much and was concerned about the photos looking dated before too long. Rita was hoping to use the brochure for years to come, and Rick felt that they should produce only enough for one year. Fred, not having a strong preference either way, suggested that they include both. Hallie suggested that they look into the pricing of stock photos versus photos taken and produced in-house, and then make a decision based on what they found out.

The project team held three more meetings with similar dynamics at play. Rita and Rick became increasingly frustrated with each other.

Understanding the Rigid PITA

It's important to realize that the Rigid PITA isn't singling out you and your views. Rigid PITAs see the world in a particular way and feel very strongly about their views, causing them to be utterly baffled when *anybody* doesn't view things in the same way. Their behavior has nothing to do with the fact that the opposing views are *your* views, and everything to do with the fact that the opposing views are not consistent with *their* views. This PITA type lacks awareness or acceptance to the widespread belief that there are many different ways to get from point A to point B. For the extreme Rigid PITA, it's "my way or the highway."

It's equally important to realize that most Rigid PITAs have always been that way; it's just part of who they are and how their mind works. As explained in chapter 3, the research of psychiatrists Thomas and Chess (1977) indicates that as people age, they maintain the temperament they demonstrated at birth. Therefore, it is likely that Rigid PITAs were born with more structured personalities and temperaments. Think about people you know, and how some tend to need a lot of structure in their lives and others sort of fly by the seat of their pants. When you go on vacation or take a trip, there are usually a few family members or friends who need to have everything scheduled and planned out in advance, whereas others just go with the flow and do whatever they feel like doing at the time.

In the workplace, you'll see a naturally structured coworker manage a meeting much differently than an unstructured one. The structured coworker will type up a detailed meeting agenda ahead of time and e-mail it to committee members to review. Then, during the meeting, the structured coworker sticks closely to the agenda and moves people along if the group is staying on any one agenda item too long. Conversely, the unstructured coworker thinks of the agenda on the way to the meeting and is fine if the group doesn't hit all agenda topics. He or she is more flexible in enabling the group to spend extra time if necessary. Both of these styles are perfectly okay when not taken to the extreme.

Obviously, Rigid PITAs fall under the structured umbrella. There is absolutely nothing wrong with being prepared and structured; in fact, it's necessary to be successful. However, when the structure turns into undue rigidity, the structured coworker turns into a Rigid PITA. Using the same meeting management example, when the structured meeting manager doesn't allow the group time to go deeper into a critically important conversation or debate because he or she is so wed to the agenda, that person becomes a Rigid PITA.

The important point to remember in all this is that a Rigid PITA was likely born with a personality and temperament that need a lot of structure and control. Understanding this reality will, we hope, help you increase your level of patience and tolerance in dealing with a rigid coworker.

Once again, remember that there are varying degrees and frequencies of all PITAs. Some Rigid PITAs dig in and hold their ground only on certain topics that they feel strongly about. Others need to have their way all the time and rarely compromise without major turmoil.

The degree of difficulty of working with a Rigid PITA can also depend on whether there are other kinds of PITAs embedded in your rigid coworker. For example, it's a lot different dealing with a Crusty Rigid PITA than it is dealing with a Soggy Rigid PITA. You always need to assess the whole PITA before planning your coping strategies.

Strategies for Coping with a Make-Your-Own (Rigid) PITA

Now that you understand Rigid PITAs a little better, you're more equipped to cope with them in the workplace. Following are several approaches and strategies for coping more effectively with Rigid PITAs.

Don't Get Defensive

As presented in the preceding section, Rigid PITAs aren't slamming your views and ways of doing things just because they're *yours*. They are disagreeing with your views and ways of doing things because they aren't *theirs*. Rigid PITAs will disagree unconditionally with anybody who has different views than theirs.

So the first step in dealing more effectively with a Rigid PITA is not to take such rigidity personally and get defensive. Nothing good typically results from acting out defensively. In other words, don't become crusty when dealing with a rigid coworker. Crusty PITAs don't usually cope very well with Rigid PITAs.

Use Honey, Not Vinegar

Taking the high road and not getting defensive allows you to approach your rigid coworkers in a more positive way. You'll get so much further with Rigid PITAs if you respect their views, express that their views are important, but tactfully offer your opposing views. Remember that Rigid PITAs feel strongly about their views on the world; these views are an important part of who they are. If you attack the PITAs' views, you are attacking *them*. And the more you attack, the deeper the Rigid PITAs dig in and stand their ground. They're like a boa constrictor: once it has you in its grasp, the more you try to move away from it, the tighter its grasp becomes. In our scenario, Rita got defensive and fought against Rick's suggestions, causing him to further tighten the grip on his views.

Compromise While Standing Your Ground

To work more effectively with a Rigid PITA, it's important to find a "middle-of-the-road" approach. You need to stay away from the two extremes. The aggressive extreme (Rita) causes the Rigid PITA to dig in deeper. Conversely, the passive approach allows the Rigid PITA to steamroll right over you and your views.

In our scenario, Fred didn't stand his ground at all. He was willing to forfeit any opinions he had on the brochure just to avoid further conflict. Hallie's approach was the best example of an effective middle-of-the-road approach. While Rita and Rick kept on fighting over which benefit should be presented first, Hallie firmly suggested starting off the brochure with healthcare benefits because three out of the four project team members thought it should be that way. But she also suggested revisiting it once the brochure layout is finished. Hallie also found a good compromise to the photos versus graphics dilemma.

Adjust Your Approach Depending on the Type of Rigid PITA

Your approach to working with a Rigid PITA will be different if, for example, your coworker is a Crusty Rigid PITA rather than a Soggy Rigid PITA. With Crusty Rigid PITAs, you'll need to be able to accept and tolerate that they may react harshly. Not only will these types of coworkers dig in deeply with what they believe, but the crust inside might cause them to be abrupt and verbally bash any opposing thoughts you have.

You'll need to be extra tough to fight off your urges to get defensive and lash back. Refer to chapter 3 and apply some of the coping strategies outlined for dealing with the Crusty PITA, especially the strategy that focuses on approaching your coworker face-to-face, individually. When dealing with a Soggy Rigid PITA, you'll need to be more sensitive when opposing views. This type of PITA is likely to get hurt if you don't choose your words carefully.

Appreciate What the Rigid PITA Brings to the Table

You should acknowledge that some good comes from the rigidity of a Rigid PITA. Most Rigid PITAs tend to be very structured and detail-oriented. They cross their *T*s and dot their *I*s. If you can get Rigid PITAs to compromise on their views or ideas, they can be valuable team members. They will follow through on tasks in a timely manner. They will bring some order to meetings and keep people on time. Rigid PITAs are also strong in organizing events or programs. Remembering these strengths might help you get through some of the frustrating moments that come from working with rigid coworkers.

When Your Direct Report Is a Rigid PITA: Tips for Managers

- Praise the person's positives prior to addressing any areas that need improvement or revisions. Because your rigid employee feels very strongly about his or her work and doing things a certain way, you'll be more likely to get him or her to bend if you first acknowledge all the good aspects.

- Focus less on the rigid employee and more on the needs of the office or organization. Your rigid employee will more likely compromise on a controversial issue if the issue is presented as a need of the office rather than some wrongdoing on his or her part. For example, if you felt that the brochure your rigid employee produced needed to be revised, focus the need for the revision on a new direction of the office rather than the employee's poor judgment.

- Tactfully confront your rigid employee regarding his or her rigidity. If you've determined that the rigidity is becoming too costly to your office and to the employee's working relationships, you're doing him or her no good by looking the other way. As mentioned before, start off this gentle confrontation by mentioning the many positive assets that your rigid employee possesses. Then provide concrete examples as to how the extreme rigidity can be detrimental to the office and to working relationships. Also clarify your expectations of him or her as you move forward. Many rigid employees need clear and precise action steps laid out in order to make positive changes.

Professionals Increasing Their Awareness: Strategies for Becoming Less Rigid

We all have the potential to be a Rigid PITA from time to time. Aren't there times when you feel strongly about a controversial issue and dig in deeply to defend your point of view? Haven't you ever become stubborn in not wanting to give up on an idea you had? Have you ever become a bit obsessive working on a special project and found yourself coming back to it over and over to make it a little better? As with all types of PITAs, the key to keeping your rigidity in check is becoming aware of your Rigid PITA tendencies.

Following are strategies for increasing your self-awareness and keeping your Rigid PITA tendencies in check.

Determine When You Are Most Likely to Be Rigid

As with all types of PITAs, the first strategy for becoming less rigid is to identify those work situations or times when you tend to become rigid. That way, you have a better chance of catching yourself the next time you're in those situations. Is there an issue or a cause that you feel strongly about where there's little room for compromise in your mind? Is there a coworker who brings out the rigidity in you? Do you have an ongoing project that you care deeply about and want to make perfect whenever you're working on it? Figure out what brings out the rigidity in you so that you can do something about it.

Pick Your Battles

Now that you've identified times at work when your rigidity tends to surface, ask yourself which situations are worth digging in on and which aren't. In the work scenario, Rick chose to continue fighting for retirement benefits to be placed first in the brochure. Was that a fight worth fighting for? Another important question to ask yourself in times of rigidity is *why* you are digging in so deep. Is it more about wanting to win the argument than about what you're arguing for? Is it something from your past that you're projecting onto your current situation?

In the scenario, why did Rick and Rita dig in so deeply? Did they actually care more about which benefit was listed where, or was it more about winning the argument? Make sure the "thing" that's causing you to be stubborn and rigid is something that has an impact on your company rather than your ego.

Create a New Recipe for Softening Your Rigid Behavior

After you identify legitimate work situations that cause you to be rigid, it's important to think of more effective ways to work through those troubling situations in less rigid ways. Following are several guidelines for softening your rigid behavior during rigid situations.

Keep Your Ego and Competitiveness in Check

As alluded to previously, there are too many times when rigid behavior is a result of one's individual ego or competitive drive rather than what's best for the company. When you find yourself holding your ground firmly in opposition to a coworker, make sure you're arguing for the betterment of the company and not the massaging of your ego. Just as brothers and sisters tend to argue just to get "one up," make sure you're not extending an argument because of the feelings you have toward a certain coworker.

Fight Fair When Holding Your Ground

When you're fighting the right battles, remember that you can hold your ground firmly without offending your coworkers. Your rigidity will be received with respect rather than resentment if you take the high road and argue your case in a more positive, less offensive way.

Listen Attentively and Openly to Opposing Viewpoints

When you feel passionately about your point of view, you might have a tendency to focus almost solely on your thoughts and responses, making it next to impossible to listen attentively to opposing coworkers. Opening your mind and attentively listening will make it possible to identify certain points that actually make sense. Taking this approach can also cause your coworkers to, in turn, become more open and attentive to *your* views. In the scenario, Rick might have gotten further with Rita if he had shown that he was open to her views.

Seek Out Mini Compromises

For those issues and arguments that you really believe are best for the company, try to find smaller compromises that won't damage the overall outcome. Losing a battle or two along the way might enable you to win the war. Your coworkers won't see you as highly rigid if you're able to give in from time to time. If Rick, for example, had been willing to let Rita win the "order of benefits" argument (since he was outnumbered, anyway), he might have had more luck in winning the "photos versus graphics" argument that came later.

Have Your "Rigid Antenna" Up at All Times

To keep yourself from regressing back to your rigid ways, you need to keep your rigid antenna up at all times. What signals do you need to be aware of that will help keep your rigid situations from getting worse? When your blood begins to boil and you find yourself getting a bit agitated, that's usually a sign that you feel strongly about the topic or issue at hand and you'll most likely dig in and hold your ground. As noted earlier, a certain coworker might bring out an excess of rigidity in you. So when you are forced to work closely with that person, activate your antenna to monitor your rigidity. If Rick's antenna had been up and running, Rita's presence might have been the signal he needed to force himself to open his mind and try to identify mini compromises.

Keep Things in Perspective

With so many major problems and concerns facing our world today, try to keep some of the smaller things in perspective. This big-picture outlook will help alleviate some of the hyper-concern or overly strong feelings you might have about certain issues or conflicts. If Rita or Rick had embraced this kind of perspective, they might have realized that which benefit was presented first wasn't all that important. While it's important to work hard and take your work seriously, don't get all worked up over issues and make them life-or-death situations. Try to save most of your emotional energy for your friends and loved ones.

CHAPTER 8

The Royal PITA:
A Pampered Prima Donna

The Royal PITA type is a little different from the others. Unlike the other PITAs, which actually sound like a type of pita you can eat (Overstuffed PITA, Sloppy PITA, and so on), the Royal PITA doesn't make sense until you sound out the acronym (Royal Pain In The Ass). This kind of PITA expects to receive the royal treatment. In a nutshell, there's a sense of entitlement among Royal PITAs. In the workplace, the extreme Royal PITA wants to have a job that is challenging, rewarding, and exciting while yielding a huge salary and plenty of leisure time. These types aren't usually willing to pay their dues; they want it all— *now!*

Royal PITAs tend to act a bit self-centered, thinking that the world revolves around them. For example, when the office needs an extra hand or somebody to staff a special program at night, Royal PITAs tend to give an excuse that they think is unique to them. But when it's time for a promotion, Royal PITAs can't imagine anybody who deserves it more than they do. Because of this self-centeredness, Royal PITAs also tend to have tunnel vision, not being as aware of what other people are thinking and feeling as they probably should be. Get the picture? Do you know anybody like this?

A Working Definition for the Royal PITA

A Royal PITA is a coworker who tends to be self-centered and spoiled and who has a sense of entitlement, expecting to get pretty much everything that he or she wants and being somewhat oblivious to how others receive him or her. Throughout this chapter, we refer to those people who display these characteristics as being "royal." We'll also refer to those situations that tend to cause royal behavior as "royal situations."

The Royal PITA at Work

You can spot Royal PITAs in a lot of different work scenarios. However, coworkers tend to show their royalness most after you've worked alongside them for a substantial period of time. In the scenario that follows, Cassandra (better known as Cassie) is a newly hired high school Biology teacher who was asked to be on a school-wide committee charged with designing a career-education program. The committee's goal is to establish a career-education program that helps its high school students to be better equipped to choose a career, find a job, and market themselves to employers or colleges. Joining Cassie on the committee are three other teachers, a school counselor, and an assistant principal, all of whom are older and more experienced than Cassie.

Famous Royal PITAs

Here are some characters from popular television shows and movies who exemplify Royal PITA characteristics:

- Charlie Sheen as Charlie Harper *(Two and a Half Men)*

- David Ogden Stiers as Maj. Charles Emerson Winchester III *(M*A*S*H)*

- Ashley Tisdale as Sharpay Evans *(High School Musical)*

- Matthew Broderick as Ferris Bueller *(Ferris Bueller's Day Off)*

- Sean Hayes as Jack McFarland *(Will & Grace)*

- Judy Reyes as Nurse Carla Espinosa *(Scrubs)*

At the first meeting, Cassie stormed right in, proposing that their high school adopt a variation of a career-education program that she participated in as a student 10 years ago. In the process of explaining the program, Cassie blasted the existing career-education curriculum without realizing that a couple of the committee members helped to develop that curriculum. Naturally, the two colleagues got defensive, trying to explain to Cassie that they had a limited staff and felt that they bought the best career-education curriculum that they could at the time. Cassie failed to put two and two together and continued to badmouth the curriculum. When the assistant principal stepped in and suggested that they take a few steps back and brainstorm ideas, Cassie responded:

> *I don't know why we need to brainstorm when we already have a well-established career-education program from one of the best high schools in the country at our fingertips! Plus, I experienced it directly as a student, and I loved it. I could get this program started without much trouble at all. Why reinvent the wheel? I have too much work to do to be starting something from scratch.*

The school counselor chimed in:

> *Cassie, I see your point. You were directly involved in a career-education program that you thought was pretty strong. Who knows, we may end up doing something very similar. But I think Larry [the assistant principal] is right. It's only the first meeting; let's take some time to talk about our goals for the program, and then see if some of the aspects of the program that you're proposing could be incorporated.*

Cassie agreed to do this, but she wasn't very open to the ideas that were thrown out on the table. Cassie began getting tired of the brainstorming session, looking at her watch multiple times. She finally excused herself 15 minutes early to get a head start on grading a stack of papers on her desk. Later that day as school let out, the assistant principal, Larry, stopped by Cassie's room to fill her in on what was discussed during the remaining part of the meeting. Larry informed Cassie that the committee decided to research several other career-education programs, including the one from her old high school. Larry asked Cassie whether she could research one of these programs in addition to the one she proposed. Cassie responded:

> *I really don't have the time right now to research these programs. I will be happy to gather materials from my high school's program, but with all of the grading I have to do, I can't really take on more than that. The other members of the committee will probably have more time than I do. Besides, why can't the secretaries help out with this kind of mundane work?*

Larry was a bit surprised by Cassie's response and unwillingness to help out, but he let it go and said that he'd check with the other committee members. When Jim, one of the other teachers on the committee, was asked whether he'd be willing to take on another school to research because Cassie was too busy, he angrily responded:

> *I'm getting a little tired of Cassie thinking that she's the only one who has to grade papers. She thinks that the school should allow her more time to grade papers during the day so she doesn't have to grade papers at night. God forbid if she takes work home and takes time away from her social life. She slams our curriculum and puts down every idea that isn't hers...and now she won't do her share in researching schools because she has too much grading to do? Wow, must be nice to have the world revolve around you!*

Larry got a similar reaction from the other committee members. As Cassie's supervisor, Larry felt obligated to share these reactions with Cassie at their next individual meeting. Cassie responded:

> *I don't think they know how important it is for me to hang out with my friends after work. It's almost dinnertime when I get home. Then I coach my Little League team two nights a week, and the other nights I need to go to the gym to get in a workout. It's usually 8 o'clock at night before I'm home for good! And I don't like to grade papers when I'm tired. I need to be more fresh.*

Larry tried not to downplay her "busy" schedule while explaining that everybody has a lot on their plates—both personally and professionally. He also brought up the fact that Cassie struck a nerve with a couple of the other committee members who were involved in developing the existing career-education curriculum. Cassie felt that they were overly sensitive and that she was just trying to speed things along by offering up a well-established program.

Cassie continued her self-centered and entitled ways during the remaining committee meetings, coming in late to a couple of meetings and leaving another one early. She actually brought a stack of papers to grade during one of the later meetings, causing further resentment among her colleagues.

Understanding the Royal PITA

A prominent characteristic of the Royal PITA is a degree of entitlement. People who have a sense of entitlement believe that it is their *right, privilege,* or *prerogative* to have certain things the way that they should have them. Simply put, entitled people believe they are owed certain things or that they deserve certain things. It's important to realize that most Royal PITAs are not aware of their entitlement tendencies because their "rights" and "privileges" have been deeply ingrained into the person they have become.

There are several possible reasons that your royal coworkers developed this sense of entitlement. Maybe they were star athletes, musicians, or scholars who always had things come easy for them, receiving special privileges due to their star status. Perhaps their parents coddled them, getting them anything that they wanted and defending them whenever a teacher or coach criticized something that they did. Or maybe they were extremely attractive and popular and built up an unusually high degree of self-confidence, becoming used to people putting them on a pedestal. Regardless of the reason, Royal PITAs feel entitled to some degree.

Another key characteristic of Royal PITAs is self-centeredness. A more psychological term for this characteristic is "egocentric," which can be helpful when trying to understand Royal PITAs a little better. The clinical definition of egocentric is "Marked by extreme concentration of attention upon oneself." As noted previously, entitled coworkers have likely been doted on by others for a long time and therefore concentrate most of their attention on themselves. Notice how many "I" statements Cassie used in the work scenario.

> *I really don't have the time right now to research these programs. I will be happy to gather materials from my high school's program, but with all of the grading I have to do, I can't really take on more than that. The other members of the committee will probably have more time than I do.*

Her attention was concentrated on *herself* and all the reasons why helping out would be tough on *her*.

It's important to point out the difference between the Royal PITA and the Overstuffed PITA when it comes to egocentrism. The Overstuffed PITA's egocentric quality tends to show itself in a more obvious, conceited, attention-seeking manner. The Royal PITA's egocentric quality tends to show itself in more of a subtle, entitled, selfish kind of way.

The self-centeredness makes it tough for the Royal PITA to put himself or herself in other people's shoes. Cassie couldn't see that it was important for her colleagues to take time to brainstorm and explore other possibilities. When she suggested to Larry that her colleagues would have more time to research other programs than she did, she clearly didn't understand that her colleagues were just as busy in their personal lives as she was. Cassie has trouble imagining anybody being busier than her. It's not that Royal PITAs are mean or antisocial; as mentioned before, they are usually unaware that they're being a Royal PITA because this behavior has been a part of who they are for a very long time.

As for all PITA types, the degrees and frequencies of Royal PITAs vary. Some coworkers are royal all the time, expecting everything to go their way. Some are royal only when they care deeply about a certain subject or initiative. Obviously, you'll have a bigger challenge working with a Royal PITA who is also crusty or overstuffed; it's easier being supportive to a Royal PITA who is more pleasant to be around. Before thinking about how to cope with a Royal PITA, determine how frequent and problematic the royalness is.

Strategies for Coping with a Royal PITA

Now that you understand the Royal PITA a little better, you're in a better position to deal with him or her more effectively as you encounter him or her in the workplace. Following are several strategies for coping more effectively with the Royal PITA.

When Your Direct Report Is a Royal PITA: Tips for Managers

- Push back on and challenge your royal employee's inaccurate perceptions. It's common for Royal PITAs to be very sure of themselves because they've been right (in their minds) so many times before. Make sure you point out these misperceptions when they occur and explain where their thinking is off. Too many royal employees haven't been challenged in the past.

- Reinforce the "can-do" attitude. Most royal employees believe that they can do anything they put their minds to (thanks to frequent praise and pats on the back). Channel this attitude to your advantage by putting royal employees in charge of appropriate projects. Set the bar high regarding the expected outcomes you convey to them.

- Confront your royal employees when necessary. When royal employees cross the line by, for example, offending or insulting other coworkers, you'll need to have a talk with them and lay out clear expectations related to treating coworkers with respect. Again, too many royal employees have gotten away with treating people any way they wanted. There comes a time when they need to realize that their previous behaviors won't be acceptable under your leadership.

Remember That the Royal PITA Means No Harm

Possibly the most important coping strategy is to constantly remind yourself that Royal PITAs usually are not consciously trying to hurt or snub anybody. Their royal tendencies have become part of their personality and everyday life, so they are not aware of how they come across to their coworkers. So don't take it personally.

The worst thing you can do is take offense and become crusty back to your royal coworkers. Keep things in perspective and remain positive in your interactions with Royal PITAs.

Don't Avoid the Royal PITA: Continue to Collaborate

A typical reaction to Royal PITAs is, "Who do they think they are? What snobs!" When forced to work with a Royal PITA on a project or committee, many coworkers try to avoid a lot of direct contact and begin isolating themselves. What's important to realize is that most Royal PITAs have been given a lot of support and nurturing, so they're used to frequent contact and collaboration. It will be very difficult to establish a positive working relationship with Royal PITAs if you keep your distance from them. Challenge yourself to hang in there through the "royal treatment" and give yourself a chance to eventually build a constructive working relationship.

Give the Royal PITA a Tactful Wake-up Call

Most Royal PITAs haven't had enough people in the past challenge their entitled tendencies. They've gotten their way too many times and have received a ton of pats on the back. This overabundance of coddling and praising has "enabled" and supported their Royal PITA behavior.

Once you have established a positive working relationship (as advised in the preceding coping strategy), don't be afraid to initiate a heart-to-heart talk with your royal coworker in an attempt to get him or her to see how such royal behavior can be detrimental at times. This can potentially serve as a wake-up call for your coworker because few if any people in his or her past have ever addressed this behavior.

When confronting your coworker, start off by pointing out all his or her positive assets and how you enjoy working with him or her. Mention that you're bringing up this issue only because you care about and respect him or her as a colleague. Acknowledge that you know your coworker doesn't intend to offend anybody, but that his or her demeanor and tone can sometimes be misinterpreted. Although it might not be pleasant for the Royal PITA to hear this, in the long run he or she will probably respect you more for bringing it up (if not now, maybe years in the future).

Look for Ways to Channel the Royal Assets

As mentioned previously, you might tend to want to create distance between you and your royal coworkers and become defensive. This defensiveness causes you to be closed-minded to thoughts and ideas coming from your royal coworkers. Try to get past this hesitance and look openly for good ideas or initiatives that your royal coworkers offer. If there is something that your royal coworker is passionate about, why not let him or her run with the idea and make positive contributions?

Most Royal PITAs *expect* to succeed. Channel this "can-do" attitude in ways that you and your coworkers will reap the benefits. Offer to help out, but allow your determined royal coworker to take the lead on certain initiatives and get things done.

Appreciate What the Royal PITA Brings to the Table

Royal PITAs have several assets that stem from their royal tendencies. As mentioned previously, royal coworkers typically have an abundance of self-confidence, expecting to reach a high level of success in whatever they do. It's nice to have this degree of optimism on your team.

Also, similar to crusty coworkers, your royal coworkers call things as they see them. You don't have to sift through the layers of tact and diplomacy to understand where the royal coworkers stand on a certain issue or topic. In today's politically correct world, this blunt and honest approach can be very refreshing.

Finally, since many Royal PITAs have become royal because they've had more success or popularity than most people, they are used to being in the limelight and having to perform "on stage."

So when you have a big-time, high-profile client or event, the royal coworker typically is very comfortable in this type of situation and usually is able to take things in stride better than most. For example, if a university is hosting a reception to honor and recognize nationally known, distinguished alumni, a royal employee might be a wise choice for saying a few words about the alumni during the formal presentation of awards.

Professionals Increasing Their Awareness: Strategies for Becoming Less Royal

We all have our times of feeling a bit entitled and self-centered. When you've been working a lot of nights and weekends, don't you want to be rewarded for your efforts? Haven't there been times when you felt strongly about something and were a bit self-centered when arguing your case? As always, the key to keeping your royalness in check is to be aware of the problem. Following are strategies for increasing your self-awareness and keeping your Royal PITA tendencies in check.

Identify Specific Times When You Feel a Sense of Entitlement

As mentioned more than once in this chapter, Royal PITAs tend to be unaware of their royal behaviors. So the first thing you must do is put your finger on those times when you feel a sense of entitlement. An entitled *feeling* is less noticeable than an obvious action or behavior. Think of those work situations when you feel you are owed something or deserve something. For example, it's common for workers to feel as though they deserve a day off after working multiple nights and weekends. It's also common for workers to believe they deserve a raise after an exceptionally productive year.

Many recent graduates tend to get impatient in their first or second job, feeling as though they aren't being challenged enough or given the level of responsibilities they deserve. They might have graduated from a prestigious college or top-ranked graduate program and believe that they are not being utilized or appreciated as much as they should be. If this is you, take a step back and realize that it takes time to earn trust, build a reputation, and work your way up the ladder.

Determine and Challenge Unjustified Feelings of Entitlement

Now that you've pinpointed times when you tend to feel a bit entitled, it's healthy to determine which feelings are justified and which ones are not. In the work scenario, Cassie should have challenged her self-imposed prerogative to grade papers during a committee meeting or leave early to grade papers. Feeling entitled to grade papers whenever she wanted and distracting herself and coworkers in the process is *not* justified. Cassie was very self-centered in thinking that she was the only committee member too busy to research other career-education programs.

Think about which of your feelings of entitlement are not justified and how your coworkers receive your corresponding behavior. Figure out ways to challenge and mitigate these unjustified feelings of entitlement.

Determine a Course of Action for Justified Entitled Feelings

For those feelings of entitlement that *are* justified, you should develop a positive game plan for getting those things you feel entitled to. In the previous example concerning recent graduates not feeling challenged and utilized well, it might be true that the organization could get much more out of them if they gave them more responsibility. If that's the case, they should channel their feelings of entitlement in a positive way by initiating a meeting with their direct supervisor to let him or her know that they're ready to take on more responsibility.

Think about constructive ways to address your justified feelings of entitlement without coming across as spoiled or self-centered. Put the company first as you explain why you should be given more responsibility (or whatever). If your supervisor isn't receptive, try to understand his or her point of view and that of the company. You might be overlooking or forgetting something that makes sense as to why you aren't getting what you think you deserve. For example, if you feel you deserve a higher salary, there may be certain equity issues that you aren't aware of that would put the company in a precarious position if you were to get a higher salary.

Become More Team-Oriented

It's natural for everyone to be self-centered to some degree. After all, we are forced to take control of our own career in order to be successful in today's competitive world of work. But some people (Royal PITAs included) take this notion too far and believe that the only way to succeed is to fight and claw their way to the top—sometimes at the expense of others. This is even more prevalent today, when there isn't the two-way loyalty that used to exist between employers and employees. So there's the feeling that, if the employer isn't looking out for my best interest, then I'm not going to be loyal to the company; rather, I'll look out for number one. Well, we strongly believe that you will perform better (and be perceived less royally) if you become more team-oriented than I-oriented.

We'll use a sports analogy to illustrate the point. Each year, the NBA honors one basketball player as the league's most valuable player (MVP). Time and time again, the MVP award hasn't gone to the most skilled player who scores the most points, but to the player who has made his team more successful. From Magic Johnson to Larry Bird to Michael Jordan and Steve Nash, they all received the MVP award when they played a big part in making their team successful. Even Michael Jordan didn't receive the MVP award until his Bulls team began winning championships.

Another compelling example—this time in the business world—is demonstrated through a recent study on leadership. From their research on executives, the global executive search firm Spencer Stuart reports that 90 percent of the most effective executives are supportive and caring about the success of their subordinates.

When you become more team oriented and strive to help your coworkers succeed, you will realize the best type of success. In the process, you'll become much less royal in the eyes of your coworkers.

Have Your "Royal Antenna" Up at All Times

As you read in previous chapters, you need to keep your antenna up at all times to detect signals of royalness coming on. You can change your royal behaviors only if you're aware of them when they're occurring. Throughout our busy workdays, we do things without thinking much about them. Signals that your royal antenna might pick up from others are resentment, anger, avoidance, and withdrawal. When you complain about something at work and act like it's all beneath you, your coworkers might be thinking what the late Chris Farley used to say, "Well, la di *fricken* dah!"

Early on, you'll most likely need to manually put up your antenna during the royal work situations you identified and be more consciously on the lookout. Eventually, your royal antenna will go up automatically and you'll sense your coworkers' reactions more quickly. In the scenario, Cassie could have used a royal antenna to receive signals of frustration and resentment from her coworkers as she graded her papers in the middle of a meeting.

CHAPTER 9

The Combo PITA:
The Worst of Several Worlds

Human beings, personality types, and behaviors are complex. Rarely can a person be captured and categorized by only one PITA type. When someone is truly a pain in the ass, he or she often possesses an array of annoyances to a sufficient degree that the Combo PITA is the best representation.

The Combo PITA concept gives you the flexibility to creatively produce the right combination of ingredients to describe and capture the PITA(s) in your life. Of course, this can take an exponential number of forms. Common Combo PITAs might be the Crusty, Overstuffed PITA; the Soggy, Sloppy PITA; or even the Royal, Make-Your-Own PITA. If you're really unfortunate, you might encounter a PITA of larger proportions—perhaps a Sealed, Crusty, Rigid PITA trio.

Whereas accurately describing and categorizing a Combo PITA in the workplace certainly presents a challenge, developing strategies to intervene and cope with a Combo PITA takes the challenge to an even higher level. In some cases, the interventions might be as systematic as combining some of the strategies for dealing with each of the separate types of PITAs to come up with a combination strategy. More often than not, you might have to draw on what you've learned about each of the PITA types to come up with a strategy that is as unique as the PITA himself or herself. After all, we are talking about human beings who are highly complex, multifaceted individuals. Although the PITA types offer general categories for describing some behavioral styles, certainly they are blunt instruments when it comes to addressing all those bothersome, hair-pulling, nail-biting behavioral nuances that reveal themselves in the workplace.

A Working Definition for the Combo PITA

A Combo PITA is a coworker who tends to show multiple PITA styles in varying combinations. In one instance you might see crusty, in another instance overstuffed, and yet another instance sealed. Or consult your own PITA menu to pick your own Combo PITA. To simplify, we refer to the people who display multiple PITA characteristics as "Combo."

The Crusty, Overstuffed, Sealed Combo PITA at Work

Consider the example of Darryl, who has the traits of a combo PITA. Darryl is a guy who has accumulated all that life can bestow on one person in terms of material wealth and power. He is a self-made man in his mid-50s who made it big in the real-estate business by buying up land, creating value out of the land by constructing office buildings and apartment complexes, and then selling the property when it could command a healthy profit. Darryl was very successful as a businessman because he knew how to spot the potential for making a dollar, he was ruthless in going after what he wanted, and he was very frugal with money.

Having been raised in a working-class family, Darryl knew what it meant to count his pennies. His father had been a jack-of-all-trades, working part of the year as a farm hand, other times working as a laborer at the grain mill, and in the winter shoveling snow out of driveways as well as delivering wood and coal. Darryl also knew what it meant to work hard from lessons learned from his father. He was expected to contribute to the family income at an early age. He sometimes worked beside his father in the field or on delivery runs. Other times he went out and hustled work on his own. From the very young age of 13, Darryl was spending his time after school, on weekends, and over holidays performing labor work for local, small-business owners.

Famous Combo PITAs

Here are some characters from popular television shows and movies who exemplify Combo PITA characteristics:

- Hugh Laurie as Dr. Gregory House (House M.D.): Crusty, Overstuffed

- Neil Patrick Harris as Barney Stinson (How I Met Your Mother): Overstuffed, Royal

- Carroll O'Connor as Archie Bunker (All in the Family): Crusty, Sealed

- Redd Foxx as Fred G. Sanford (Sanford and Son): Crusty, Sloppy

- Marcia Cross as Bree Van De Kamp Hodge (Desperate Housewives): Rigid, Sealed

- Tim Allen as Tim "The Toolman" Taylor (Home Improvement): Sloppy, Overstuffed

Darryl was always a very competent worker. Regardless of the task, he was known as someone who got the job done, got it done on time, and often did it under budget. He was definitely a "go-to" guy when it came to seeking out young help from the community. He was always working when other boys were "indulging" in after-school sports, hunting, or fishing on the local lake. Although Darryl may have wanted to take part in these types of boyhood activities at one time, he learned from his father that recreational activities were for lazy people and they were consistently forbidden.

Over time, Darryl adopted his father's views on the high meaning of work while having little regard for recreational time, taking weekends and holidays off, or even spending time with friends and family. By his high school and college years, he was a serious student, had developed a strong sense of entrepreneurship, and had spent much of his time scheming ways to get wealthy. It was no surprise that he ultimately chose to major in business management at the state university.

Classmates who knew Darryl always had the sense that he would be the head of his own company because they thought he could never work for anyone else. Darryl was viewed as highly independent and a man who needed to be in control. He was quick to anger in many interpersonal situations and generally could not handle being challenged on issues or disagreed with. People generally regarded him as a bully because he resorted to verbal criticism and intimidation when someone disagreed with his perspective on just about anything.

If people could align themselves with Darryl's value system, they could win his favor. He needed lots of strokes, so people had to convey the message that they admired and respected him. When in his presence around others, people had to be careful not to draw too much attention to themselves. He would get noticeably irritated when attention shifted to another person, and he was aggressively able to switch the attention back to himself. Essentially, if an employee lived his work life to serve the needs of Darryl, he or she would become a prized and valued employee. If that employee began to express individual needs or to strive for individual accomplishments, his or her relationship with Darryl would soon become strained. Although Darryl was wealthy, accomplished, and respected as a capable businessman, he was competitive and jealous when anyone else pursued and achieved a noteworthy goal.

One example is the case of a long-time employee, Harriet, who was a devoted accountant in Darryl's businesses. Harriet was always loyal to Darryl. He trusted her with all the financial information within his expansive business network. She was very skilled with numbers and financial analysis, and her dutiful work habits and financial savvy made Darryl a tremendous amount of money over the years. She literally made Darryl millions through her sophisticated knowledge of money management, tax law, and investments. Harriet was paid as well as anyone in Darryl's organization, but pay was average at best and raises were modest even for his best employees. Harriet was well aware that her compensation was lagging behind market standards, yet she hadn't changed jobs due to her comfort level with the organization, her sense of loyalty to Darryl, and her fear of making a change.

Harriet's answer to her quandary was to start a tax and bookkeeping service on the side that she ran in the evenings and on weekends. She also completed a bachelor's degree in accounting while working for Darryl, which his company funded at the rate of 50 percent tuition. As business continued to increase for Harriet over a five-year period, she was unable to keep up with her workload.

She knew it was time to have a heart-to-heart conversation with Darryl about leaving the company to pursue her lifetime dream of running and owning her own business.

Harriet knew she had to be delicate about the conversation for many reasons, but primarily because she had revealed little to Darryl about her private business over the past five years. She knew Darryl could react negatively, and she needed to work for three more months in order to make a few arrangements to allow for a smooth transition.

As anticipated, Darryl was furious! "How could you betray me like this? How dare you go behind my back and start something like this without me knowing about it?" Harriet sat quietly as he continued with his tirade. He continued, "All you do is look out for yourself and think about making money. Well, good luck because I don't think that your skills as an accountant are that good, anyway. After all, I made you what you are today." Harriet kept her cool during his outburst. When he was finished, she commented, "I don't understand why you are so angry. After all, I am only doing the same thing and following the same path that you once started down many years ago. You have your own business, so why can't I?" reasoned Harriet.

Darryl did not respond well to her sensible attempt at logic and compassion. It only frustrated him further. He proceeded to kick her out of his office. "Clean out your office and leave the premises right away" was his final statement to her. After Harriet left the organization, Darryl spent the next two months badmouthing and ridiculing Harriet for her betrayal and for her "selfish entrepreneurial scheming."

Understanding the Combo Crusty, Overstuffed, Sealed PITA

It is crucially important to emphasize that the Combo PITA type is complicated to understand but probably most representative of problematic personalities. Human beings are multidimensional, personalities are combo by their very nature, and every individual needs to be conceptualized and handled differently. That being said, Darryl's case is probably one that you recognize. Many people probably either work with or know of a Darryl.

So what drives Darryl? He obviously has very intense needs to be the person in power, to have as many resources as possible, to expect and demand loyalty from his employees, and to be in control of his organization and everyone in it. He gets angry when people challenge his power, he gets jealous and agitated when others are equally as or more accomplished than he is, and he responds well when people live and work to serve his needs.

No doubt Darryl was profoundly impacted by his father's work ethic and his approach to earning and accumulating money. His PITA behavior has been reinforced over the years by the successes he has experienced as a businessman and the results that he has gotten by using intimidation, fear, and domination in keeping and coercing his employees. Although Darryl might be disliked, disrespected, or even despised by his employees, he has managed to achieve results through his own form of coercion and wielding of power.

Unfortunately, working for a man like Darryl creates few options. He is rigid in his approach to leading people. He sets up a no-win situation where he is right; if you disagree, you are wrong. There is no room for multiple viewpoints in Darryl's thinking. It is also highly unlikely that Darryl is going to change or even slightly alter

his way of thinking because he does not give enough consideration to the fact that he has a negative impact on people. He is
closed off to self-awareness and thus he is a true Sealed PITA in
addition to his other PITA features.

In the same way that a beaten-down spouse is controlled by an
abusing partner or children are kept in check by punitive parents,
Darryl's employees have no doubt learned that the way to survive
and thrive is to perform well, to stay quiet, to do everything they
are told, and to make the boss look good. They should not engage
in individual pursuits or better themselves in ways that might capture Darryl's attention and tap into his insecurities or jealousy.

A psychological understanding of why Darryl is a Crusty,
Overstuffed, Sealed PITA is complex. It might not necessarily be
useful for the people who have to work with these PITAs everyday; however, it is important to know what motivates them, what
they value, where they bend, where they hold firm, what you can
tolerate, and how much these PITAs infuriate you. In the end, the
analysis is as much about you and your reactions to Crusty,
Overstuffed, Sealed PITAs as it is about the PITAs themselves.

Strategies for Coping with the Combo Crusty, Overstuffed, Sealed PITA

The approach and technique for coping with Darryl and other
Crusty, Overstuffed, Sealed Combo PITAs like him are choice
based:

- You understand his value system, what motivates him, how
  he acts and reacts, and what he rewards and you *choose* to
  work within that system; OR

- You choose to disagree with the "Darryl-like" way of conducting business and treating people, yet stay engaged anyway for the sake of meeting your own needs for employment; OR

- You leave Darryl and the Crusty, Overstuffed, Sealed system altogether.

You do have control over how you cope with PITAs like Darryl, even though on the surface you might feel powerless. Because it's highly unlikely that Darryl will change due to the sealed nature of his personality, the options are straightforward.

For the sake of consistency, let's assume that the Combo PITA is the head or chief of your organization, unit, team, or division, although this type of Combo PITA could represent anyone at any level of power or any position in your work life. We assume that this person is in a position of power because it's unlikely that workers with limited power could get away with acting this way. They would normally be terminated or forced to change out of fear of losing their jobs.

So how do you cope with such a difficult person? How do you put things into perspective for yourself? Because this type of PITA is a combo of several PITA types, you could refer to many of the strategies we've offered for each of the individual PITAs. It's likely that the strategies listed for the individual Sealed, Overstuffed, and Crusty PITAs can also be used here. For particularly difficult Combo PITAs, here are some additional strategies for you to try.

Adopt an In-Control/Out-of-Control Perspective

While coping with a Combo PITA can be extremely difficult, it helps to know those parts of your job (and the PITA) that you can control and those aspects that you cannot. After a while, you start to understand those aspects of the PITA that might be workable and changeable and those aspects that are not. Let go of the things that you cannot change. It doesn't help to stress or fret over these parts of the job or the PITA's personality that are out of your control.

Many people get worked up more than necessary because they continue to be frustrated and angry that things aren't different. Focus on the aspects of your position, aspects of yourself, or even aspects of the PITA where you may have some control. Anyone working in close contact with a Combo PITA probably has some sense about what these areas might be.

Learn to Disconnect Yourself Emotionally from the Combo PITA

PITAs like Darryl can make people very angry because they generally have little regard for other people's feelings. Remember that this is not a personal attack on you as an individual. As with the Crusty PITA, don't take the Combo PITA's attitude and behaviors personally. Most of the time, the PITA's extreme reactions to workplace events have nothing at all to do with you personally, even though it can feel that way.

Once you can keep your own emotions out of your interactions with the Combo PITA, the less aggravated you will get over time. In the end, it's important to stay calm and level in the midst of the Combo PITA's fury instead of reacting and saying something that you wish you hadn't. Although it might feel good to let the

Combo PITA have a piece of your mind, in the end you will most likely regret that you didn't handle the situation more calmly.

Stay Centered

Attempt to stay centered throughout your day, particularly during times when you interact frequently with the Combo PITA. Centering techniques may include the following:

- **Deep-breathing exercises:** Deep breathing is a method for calmly slowing down your breathing. It requires moving the air in and out of your diaphragm area (watch your stomach go in and out). Try counting to four as you inhale, holding for a count of two, and counting to four as you exhale.

- **Positive self-talk:** Positive self-talk is a way to counteract negative messages you might be receiving from Combo PITAs. Examples could be "I am a skilled and useful worker," "I have the right to be treated with respect on the job," or "I always have choices about the ways I react and respond."

- **Imagery:** Imagery entails putting yourself in a place that is relaxing or a place that enhances your self-esteem in some way. You may choose to place yourself at the beach under the warm sun, or you might visualize yourself in a time when you felt the most smart, the most competent, or the most successful.

People respond differently to these techniques. Some people prefer the physical tension relief associated with deep-breathing exercises, whereas others prefer the mental calming associated with affirming self-talk or positive imagery. The beauty of all these techniques is that you can engage in them at your desk, over lunch, or anyplace where you can mentally escape for a few minutes. (But if you perform surgery or drive a truck, please refrain from trying these centering techniques until the end of the work day!)

Make Sure That You Have Multiple Ways to Keep Your Self-Esteem Intact

Your feelings about yourself as a competent and valued employee could take a beating in the regular presence of the Combo PITA. You will need protection so that your self-esteem does not suffer too much. The best way to protect your self-esteem is to put plenty of activities in your life that help you to feel good about yourself. The type of activity doesn't really matter as long as you get a good feeling about your own abilities and competence as the result of engaging in them. Try to get involved in constructive workplace activities in addition to recreational activities at home.

For example, you might be a highly talented event planner, so you decide to organize the company picnic and other human resources–sponsored activities within your organization. At home, you might play tennis and belong to a book club because you enjoy them and you feel competent when you do them. The point here is that it's best not to invest all your self-esteem in your job. This is a good idea in general, but particularly when you are involved daily with a Crusty, Overstuffed, Sealed PITA.

Appreciate What the Combo PITA Brings to the Table

The Combo PITA's contribution will depend on the PITA types that make up the combo. The best way to assess a Combo PITA's positive qualities is to reflect on the individual PITAs in the preceding chapters and pull together some concepts. However, we acknowledge that the whole is often more than the sum of its parts, so stay open to other positive features that we might not have mentioned in earlier chapters. After all, much of PITA behavior is learned, and some of these behaviors must have been useful in the Combo PITA's professional journey.

Professionals Increasing Their Awareness: The Potential of Crusty, Overstuffed, Sealed PITAs

The following is a demonstration of how a different outcome could have occurred if Darryl had been more of a "professional increasing his awareness." Although many of the individual strategies have been presented before for increasing awareness, this example helps bring them together.

It's unfortunate that Darryl has so many PITA types working against him because it requires hard work to change even one PITA style. Like many PITAs in our work lives, Darryl is a skilled guy and certainly a valuable human being, but his interpersonal deficits overshadow his effectiveness in other areas. Although Darryl has been monetarily successful in business, no doubt the cost to his employees and his employee retention has been enormous.

Let's revisit the case of Harriet to illustrate how Darryl might have changed his approach and response in a way that the course of events could have been changed. First of all, it's hard to know whether Harriet would have pursued her own business in the first place if Darryl had been more willing to fairly compensate her and make her feel more like a valued employee. Unfortunately, PITAs like Darryl are more interested in the bottom line and the hard-and-fast rules of profit-and-loss than they are invested in retaining employees and keeping them content. Most respected leaders are able to attend to both the financial and the people sides of an organization. They understand that the two are interconnected, and that both need attention for an organization to work properly.

If Darryl could have been more interpersonally aware of the people side of his organization, he might have been able to ward off Harriet's decision to leave before it was too late. The interaction with Harriet could have gone something like this:

> **Harriet:** "Darryl, I have been considering leaving the company to run my tax and bookkeeping firm full-time. I realize that I have kept my private business hidden from you, but I was certain that you would not approve. It has now grown into a sizeable business and I think I'm going to make a go of it full-time."

Darryl, who was *aware* that his anger was building, took a deep breath and paused a moment. Instead of blasting Harriet, as he normally would have, he responded as follows:

> **Darryl:** "Harriet, I am disappointed that you didn't share this information with me sooner, but I think I understand why you might not have done so. I am concerned about your contentment as an employee of my company, so I want to assist in any way I can. Please tell me a little more about your business, if you don't mind."

If we look closely into this type of response, we can see that Darryl demonstrated awareness on a number of levels. He knew that he typically gets angry when people consider leaving his organization, so he chose to take a breath and pause a moment. This level of awareness and the fact that he caught himself is enormous! The act of *taking a breath* and *pausing* may be one of the most important two steps that any Crusty, Overstuffed, Sealed PITA could take.

Second, he didn't scold; instead, he demonstrated awareness that it's hard for employees to come to him with certain kinds of information. This response serves to help relax Harriet so that she can talk openly and not feel like she will be attacked.

Third, Darryl showed a willingness to be helpful, which would ideally evolve out of an awareness that you catch more flies with honey than with vinegar. In the end, Darryl was able to delay his natural instinct to attack and scold because he had developed an awareness that this way of reacting is not helpful and not best for his organization. Heightened awareness leads to more control over reactions.

If Darryl had worked on his interpersonal awareness, it is easy to imagine that the conversation could have continued in the following manner:

> **Harriet:** "Well, it's a business that I have been running out of my home for the past five years now. As you know, I have been taking classes in accounting, and I started with some small bookkeeping and tax clients who were mostly friends and close acquaintances. I must have done a good job because they told their friends and business has really grown."

> **Darryl:** "Harriet, I'm not surprised that the business has gone well for you because you are a conscientious worker and you always do a good job. I'm aware that I don't tell you this frequently enough. I am of course wondering

whether you are happy with your current job and if there is anything that we can do to keep you employed here. Are you willing to talk about any possible options for staying on board?"

Notice that Darryl's comments and questions are not lengthy, and they don't require much eloquence in terms of how he has to word things. He merely demonstrates validation that Harriet is valued as an employee and concern that she is leaving and is potentially not happy. Darryl is not kicking her out the door, nor is he giving away the farm, but he has shown an openness and willingness to understand Harriet's situation. He was able to put on hold his own impulses to punish her in the interest of her career satisfaction and ultimately the running of his business.

The Path to Self-Awareness Takes Lots of Work

We have emphasized many times throughout this book that people and PITAs are unique and the journey toward PITA avoidance is specific to individuals. It's clear, however, that if you are in danger of becoming a Combo PITA of the Crusty, Overstuffed, Sealed variety, you have missed many, many cues along the way that your interpersonal style is not working as well as it could. At some point, you've got to begin paying attention to other people's reactions to you and caring about the things going on around you. If you have Combo PITA tendencies, paying attention, noticing people, and being more aware of your impact on people will probably create some discomfort for you because you typically ignore or disregard these areas. It's not easy to explore and come to terms with the fact that you might have a consistently negative impact on work relationships.

Coming to terms with problematic interpersonal interactions takes guts. Realizing that you have unwanted behaviors takes an honest evaluation of your present and past work relationships. This means really considering direct or indirect feedback you might have received from people in your work life; it means reflecting on the people who might have disengaged from you in some way (for example, quit, transferred, found other jobs) but who might have been valued colleagues at one time; and it means honestly noticing whether your coworkers are approaching you or avoiding you in your day-to-day work life interactions. You might not be confronted or challenged very much if you are the supervisor or leader in your organization, but you certainly will be avoided if your personality is too toxic for people to engage.

If you don't care about the quality of your work relationships, pursuing the path of the Combo PITA might be a satisfactory choice. Being sealed means never having to own responsibility for personal behavior, being overstuffed means never having to give another person credit or attention for a job well done, and being crusty means that you can bark at people and intimidate them into giving in to you most of the time.

For some people, this behavior might sound attractive because there are immediate and superficial gains to be made by going down the Combo PITA path. Yet, experience has shown that the drawbacks start to outweigh the benefits. It's a lonely work life, and even a lonely personal life, for this type of PITA. Even the Combo PITA starts to miss the connectedness and camaraderie of having close coworkers who share the desire to do a good job together as a team and who enjoy positive relationships in their work settings.

How to Become Less of a Combo PITA

Because the specific combination of each Combo PITA is unique, we won't offer generic strategies for increasing awareness and becoming less of a Combo PITA. In chapter 11, you will identify your unique Combo PITA tendencies and, through a series of probing questions, select the PITA or combination of PITAs that you most identify with. Then you will be able to complete exercises to identify work settings where your PITA tendencies come to life. Finally, you'll have the opportunity to construct strategies to help you change your PITA behaviors and responses within these specific work settings.

CHAPTER 10

A Sampler Platter of Honorable-Mention PITAs

A s we began to unveil the different kinds of PITAs through conversations with colleagues and friends and when presenting PITA seminars, people frequently came up to us and proposed additional types of PITAs that we should consider. Well, after careful consideration, we selected 10 "Honorable-Mention PITAs" that we decided to include in our book. These mini-PITAs don't make an entire meal or deserve their own chapter, but they provide good "food for thought" something to "chew on." Consider them to be "appetizers" rather than the main course.

We won't go into great depth explaining each of the Honorable-Mention PITAs (no coping strategies or work scenarios), but we'll give you enough of a taste to see whether you recognize anybody (including parts of yourself) who fits the description. We hope you enjoy sampling our platter of mini-PITAs!

The Moldy PITA

The Moldy PITA is that coworker who is resistant to change, hiding out in his or her office doing the same old, same old. You'll hear the Moldy PITA say things like, "We tried that 10 years ago and it didn't work," or "Today we rely way too much on technology," or "Why fix it if it ain't broken?" Moldy PITAs complain and drag their feet when it comes to things such as training seminars, conferences, and other forms of professional development. They tend to get stale in their jobs and bored due to not only doing the same things, but doing the same things in the same way. The worst Moldy PITAs are those who stifle creativity and who treat innovative coworkers in a patronizing way. In an age of constant change greatly due to technology, moldy coworkers can certainly be big PITAs!

Famous Moldy PITAs

- Harry Shearer as Mr. Burns *(The Simpsons)*
- Stephen Root as Milton Waddams *(Office Space)*

The Cheesy PITA

Cheesy PITAs are those who make your stomach turn by constantly using all the cheesy, catch-phrase-of-the-year words like "synergy" or "seamless transition." Here's a snapshot of the Cheesiest PITA in action:

> *I find it imperative that we **think outside the box** in generating lasting solutions **24/7. Empowering** our coworkers to experience a **seamless transition** is **paramount**. We need to be **proactive** in offering **cutting-edge** resources to our growing customer base. At our upcoming convention, the primary **take-away** must focus on **synergy** among our colleagues around the globe.*

Less annoying Cheesy PITAs overuse famous or popular business sayings, always starting with "You know what they say…'Don't sell the steak, sell the sizzle,'" or "It's not *what* you know, it's *who* you know," or "Actions speak louder than words," or "Honesty is the best policy." Other less-annoying Cheesy PITAs steal famous lines from the movies or TV and incorporate them way too often: "Is that your final answer?" "No soup for you," "Wassup?" or "Yada, yada, yada."

And then there are the everyday clichés such as "Nip it in the bud," "Spill the beans," "Who let the cat out of the bag?" "Too much on my plate," "Six of one, half-dozen of another," "Workin' hard or hardly workin'?" and "Take it with a grain of salt."

Actually, except for the "catch–phrase-of-the-year" sayings, none of these are really annoying unless they're used too frequently.

Famous Cheesy PITAs

- Ed Helms as Andy Bernard *(The Office)*

- Rob Schneider as the "making copies" guy *(Saturday Night Live)*

The Hot-n-Spicy PITA

Hot-n-Spicy PITAs arc those coworkers who are overly dramatic and highly emotional. Everything's a major moment and a big deal. You know who I'm talking about. They use five explanation points after every sentence in their e-mails. They start many sentences with dramatic warnings such as "Are you sitting down?" or "You are *not* going to believe this" or "Oh, my gosh…wait till you hear this!" And after hearing any kind of news, they respond with things like "Wow…this is soooo big!" or "Get out of here!" or "Are you dying inside?"

Some Hot-n-Spicy PITAs overuse every synonym for "great." Here are a dozen "great" synonyms you might catch them spouting: *outstanding, wonderful, amazing, tremendous, spectacular, exceptional, incredible, fantastic, awesome, magnificent, remarkable, fabulous.* When you ask them how something turned out or how their weekend was, they'll toss around these words all over the place: "I had such an amazing weekend! The movie that I saw was incredible, and the dinner beforehand was magnificent! It was literally the most marvelous night of my life!!!!!"

Famous Hot-n-Spicy PITAs

- Kirstie Alley as Rebecca Howe *(Cheers)*
- Mindy Kaling as Kelly Kapoor *(The Office)*

The Loaded PITA

Loaded PITAs are involved in *everything* and can't say "no" to anything. They are the first ones to volunteer to serve on committees because they want to have their hands in everything. They take on too much in their personal lives as well and constantly remind you how chaotic their life is, but the reality is that they thrive on chaos.

You'll find Loaded PITAs saying things like "I have way too much on my plate right now" or "I'm just trying to keep my head above water." And they love it when you validate their overloaded lifestyle by saying something like "I don't know how you keep all these balls in the air at the same time…you are juggling so many things." Because Loaded PITAs are spread way too thin, they often (unintentionally) let things fall through the cracks. You'll also see Loaded PITAs frantically running late to meetings and programs, usually giving excuses based on how busy they are.

Famous Loaded PITA

- John Cleese as Basil Fawlty *(Fawlty Towers)*

The To-Go PITA

Similar to Loaded PITAs, To-Go PITAs are constantly on the run. The difference, however, is that To-Go PITAs aren't on the run because they took on too much; they're on the run because they were born this way and know only one speed: high gear. Many people refer to To-Go PITAs as "social butterflies," bouncing from person to person and from place to place without hanging around in one spot for any length of time.

To-Go PITAs will give you the time of day as long as somebody more interesting doesn't enter the room. They'll tend to cut you off midstream when somebody "more important" catches their eye. It's extremely hard to keep their attention. To-Go PITAs are famous for asking questions and leaving before the answer is fully presented. To-Go PITAs behave a lot like reporters at the Oscars: While interviewing one actor, the reporter is constantly scoping the scene, trying to spot a more famous actor or actress coming up to the red carpet.

Famous To-Go PITA

- Kiefer Sutherland as Jack Bauer *(24)*

The Porta-PITA

Just like a porta-potty, the Porta-PITA is full of crap. Porta-PITAs exaggerate points, embellish stories, and make lame excuses. Somehow, every program or project that Porta-PITAs are involved in turns out to be "the best ever" in their eyes. From the number of people in attendance, to the quality of the food, to the type of feedback from participants—the Porta-PITA embellishes all aspects.

Porta-PITAs use a lot of "absolute" phrases, such as "College students do that *all* the time" or "*Everybody* used to do it that way." Porta-PITAs will take one person's opinion and stir up concern by saying, "People are starting to complain about..." or "I'm starting to hear some grumbling about...." According to Porta-PITAs, one person doing something one time constitutes a "trend."

One more thing: Don't believe the statistical estimates coming from Porta-PITAs. They love to report numbers that are twice the size of the actual figure: "We had more than 150 people who showed up at our event," when maybe it was more like a couple dozen.

Famous Porta-PITA

- John Ratzenberger as Cliff Clavin *(Cheers)*

The BLT PITA

The BLT PITA is part of the Cheesy PITA family. But instead of using annoying catch phrases, the BLT PITA annoys people by overusing acronyms, making everything sound like alphabet soup. It's not so much the mainstream acronyms that annoy people (such as FYI, TMI, TBA, ASAP, or AKA). And those who use a lot of text-messaging acronyms (such as LOL, AML, BRB, SYT, GTG, or LMAO) aren't the worst kind of BLT PITAs, either. What really puts the "PITA" in the BLT PITA are those cheesy acronyms that companies develop in-house to more "creatively" name a new program or initiative. Here are a few (fictional) examples of more annoying acronyms created by BLT PITAs:

EDGE (Empowering Dedicated Gardeners Everywhere)

ACE (Accelerating and Cultivating Enthusiasm)

WIG (Women Initiating Greatness)

By the way, there actually are some good acronyms out there; "PITA"—just to give you an example—is a pretty cool one, don't you think?

Famous BLT PITA

- Gary Cole as Bill Lumberg (*Office Space*)

The Overcooked PITA

Overcooked PITAs belabor points, beat things into the ground, and overanalyze everything. Due to their long-winded responses, you start to avoid asking Overcooked PITAs questions because you know it's going to be 15 minutes before you'll be able to get back to work. Overcooked PITAs also have the annoying habit of prefacing what they're about to say:

> *Before I tell you what she said, it's important that you remember that this is just one opinion, and if we had asked five other people, we probably would have gotten five different responses. So please don't overreact to what I'm about to tell you.*

All the while, you're thinking to yourself, "Oh my God…just say it already!" Overcooked PITAs will analyze decisions to death, no matter how trivial they are. Ask an Overcooked PITA what you and your office mates should order for lunch, and you'll receive a dissertation on the pros and cons of the various takeout restaurant options in town.

The Mushroom PITA

Just as mushrooms grow best and flourish in the dark, Mushroom PITAs like to keep their coworkers "in the dark" on many topics. They do this out of insecurity and the need for power because, as you know, information *is* power. You see, if Mushroom PITAs hoard important information, you and your coworkers are forced to come back to them to retrieve the information you need to do your job. When you ask Mushroom PITAs for information, they will give you only what is absolutely necessary.

In today's world of modern technology, where there are unlimited ways to make information accessible and user-friendly, there's simply no excuse for hoarding information. But Mushroom PITAs will continue to hoard, because it's in their best interest. For example, if a tax accountant provides his clients with all the information necessary to do their own taxes, the clients will stop coming back to him to do their taxes. Similarly, a Mushroom PITA plumber isn't going to give you tips to prevent plumbing-related problems from occurring. He'd rather hoard the information and advice so that you're forced to call on him to fix even the simplest problems.

The Edgy PITA

Edgy PITAs frequently say things that are on the verge of being inappropriate or politically incorrect. They like to push the envelope on controversial issues and delicate topics such as sex, race, and politics, making you feel uncomfortable being in their company. During lunches and other social situations at work, the Edgy PITA tells touchy jokes that put people in a tough spot and essentially a no-win situation. If you laugh, you might be encouraging or enabling the Edgy PITA's inappropriate humor. But if you don't laugh, you might be perceived as Mr. or Ms. Goody Two Shoes.

When the Edgy PITA is an older coworker, you often rationalize his or her edgy behavior as a "generational thing." The Edgy PITA tends to minimize the importance of being inclusive or reaching out to various underrepresented groups. Whether intentional or generational, an edgy coworker can be a real PITA to be around in today's diverse work force.

Famous Edgy PITAs

- Drew Carey as Drew Carey (*The Drew Carey Show*)
- Steve Carell as Michael Scott (*The Office*)

CHAPTER 11

Assessing and Determining Your PITA Profile

U p to this point, you've been exposed to a variety of different PITAs that you might have to work with and try to avoid becoming. We described seven main-menu PITAs (as well as the Combo):

- Sealed
- Crusty
- Overstuffed
- Soggy
- Sloppy
- Make-Your-Own (Rigid)
- Royal

We also gave you a sample of 10 Honorable-Mention PITAs:

- Moldy
- Cheesy
- Hot-n-Spicy
- Loaded
- To-Go

- Porta

- BLT

- Overcooked

- Mushroom

- Edgy

We've given you some general coping strategies to help you deal more effectively with each type of main-menu PITA, as well as some strategies to lessen your tendency to behave like any of these PITAs.

In this chapter, it's time to roll up your sleeves and start sifting through all of the PITAs in order to put your finger on the following:

- The PITA coworkers who present you the biggest challenge

- The PITA types that you have more potential to behave like at times

- The PITA types that are potentially most problematic due to your chosen career field and work situation

Generating this personalized "PITA Profile" will enable you to become the best kind of PITA—Professionals Increasing Their Awareness—and pinpoint the areas that need the most attention. All of this leads you perfectly to the last chapter, "A Personal Approach to PITA Change," where you'll learn about change strategies to help you manage your PITA Profile to your advantage and start enhancing your various working relationships and your overall work performance.

In the latter part of this chapter, you'll also have some fun determining which Honorable-Mention PITAs are most annoying to work with and which ones you have the most tendency toward being.

It is *extremely important* to point out that the purpose of the informal surveys presented in this chapter is simply to allow you to reflect on your own behaviors and tendencies. The surveys are *not* formalized instruments that have been validated in the workplace. This is *not* an exact science by any stretch but is a method to help you think more closely about how the PITA styles apply to you. Use your judgment and self-knowledge to determine how accurate the "scores" are across the surveys. You are the final judge!

Part 1: Assessing and Determining PITA Coworker Types That Present the Biggest Challenge

Although we presented coping strategies for all seven main-menu types of PITAs, it's important to realize that you won't cope equally with all types. There are "degrees of coping difficulty" that you need to examine to determine which specific PITA types present you the biggest challenge. Your ability to cope depends greatly on the type of person you are and the chemistry you have with different types of people.

For example, for those who tend to be organized and who value structure at work, the Sloppy PITA will be one of the more challenging types of PITAs to work with. Likewise, for those who are more sensitive and who value harmony, the Crusty PITA will be a difficult type of coworker to get along with. So, for this first part of building your PITA Profile, you'll need to take an honest look at yourself to more accurately determine which types of PITAs give you the biggest challenge.

Part 1: PITA Types Presenting the Biggest Challenge to Work With

For each of the five questions that follow, record a **6** next to the letter that best describes you, a **5** next to the letter that describes you next best, a **4** next to the letter that describes you next best after that, and so on. Note that you will enter a **0** next to the last letter remaining and the one that least describes you. After completing the five questions, you will be asked to compute the total sum for each PITA type. To avoid influencing your answers, do not look ahead to the scoring system until you're done answering the questions. Once you determine the PITA types that present you with the biggest challenge, it will be helpful to refer back to the corresponding PITA chapters to remind yourself of those PITAs' characteristics.

Sample

I find it difficult to work with people who

a. __3__ are high-maintenance

b. __1__ are negative and cynical

c. __6__ are self-absorbed

d. __0__ get defensive

e. __4__ are disorganized

f. __2__ are caught up with power and status

g. __5__ are rigid and inflexible

1. I find it difficult to work with people who

    a. _____ are high-maintenance

    b. _____ are negative and cynical

    c. _____ are self-absorbed

    d. _____ get defensive

    e. _____ are disorganized

    f. _____ are caught up with power and status

    g. _____ are rigid and inflexible

2. It is frustrating working with people who

    a. _____ are never on time and who turn in things late

    b. _____ won't bend or compromise

    c. _____ don't share the credit for our successes

    d. _____ need constant reassurance and support

    e. _____ feel entitled and expect special treatment

    f. _____ don't own their mistakes

    g. _____ are pessimistic

(continued)

(continued)

3. I don't enjoy working with people who

   a. _____ aren't open to feedback

   b. _____ won't make the same sacrifices that the rest of the team members make

   c. _____ are overly particular and picky

   d. _____ are brutally honest and insensitive

   e. _____ are full of themselves and conceited

   f. _____ ramble on and can't stick to agendas

   g. _____ are overly sensitive and fragile

4. I get annoyed with coworkers who

   a. _____ criticize more than they compliment

   b. _____ don't attend to details

   c. _____ can't admit to having weaknesses

   d. _____ are always seeking attention

   e. _____ overreact to the little things

   f. _____ see the world in absolute terms

   g. _____ aren't willing to pay their dues

5. I have a difficult time addressing issues and concerns with a

   a. _____ Rigid PITA

b. _____ Overstuffed PITA

c. _____ Soggy PITA

d. _____ Royal PITA

e. _____ Sealed PITA

f. _____ Crusty PITA

g. _____ Sloppy PITA

Part 1 Scoring

Refer to the five-question survey you just completed and write the numbers in the correct columns in the following table. For example, if you entered a "3" on the line next to "d" for question #1, you would write a "3" in the table for PITA #1— Sealed PITA, Question 1. Add each of the seven columns. Those with the highest scores are most likely the PITA types that present you the biggest challenge to work with.

Question	PITA #1: Sealed	PITA #2: Crusty	PITA #3: Over-stuffed	PITA #4: Soggy	PITA #5: Sloppy	PITA #6: Rigid	PITA #7: Royal
1	d = ___	b = ___	f = ___	a = ___	e = ___	g = ___	c = ___
2	f = ___	g = ___	c = ___	d = ___	a = ___	b = ___	e = ___
3	a = ___	d = ___	e = ___	g = ___	f = ___	c = ___	b = ___
4	c = ___	a = ___	d = ___	e = ___	b = ___	f = ___	g = ___
5	e = ___	f = ___	b = ___	c = ___	g = ___	a = ___	d = ___
TOTAL							

Part 2: Assessing and Determining Your Own PITA Potential and Tendencies

Just as some PITA types are tougher to work with than others, you'll have greater potential or tendencies to behave like certain PITA types more so than others. For example, if you are extremely organized and like a lot of structure, there's more potential for you to behave like a Rigid PITA at times than a Sloppy PITA. Likewise, if you are more sensitive and thin-skinned, you'll have more potential of behaving like a Soggy PITA than a Crusty PITA during certain work situations.

So, for this second part of building your PITA Profile, you'll need to (again) take an honest look at yourself to more accurately determine your potential for behaving like certain types of PITAs. While you're answering the following questions, it will be helpful to refer back to the corresponding PITA chapters to remind yourself of the PITA characteristics.

My PITA Profile

Part 2: My PITA Potential and Tendencies

Use the following scale to enter the number that most closely reflects your feelings. After answering all of the questions, you will be instructed on how to compute the total sum for each PITA type. *It's important to realize that higher scores do NOT mean that you ARE that type of PITA, but that you have some potential behaviors that you might need to monitor during certain work situations.* Please try to be as honest and introspective as possible, remembering that no one gets to see your ratings but you. Again, do not look ahead to the scoring system until you have finished answering the questions.

1—Strongly Disagree

2—Disagree

3—Slightly Agree

4—Agree

5—Strongly Agree

Part 2 Survey

1. _____ Being organized is not one of my greatest strengths.

2. _____ I primarily respect people of power and status.

3. _____ I like to plan everything out in advance and I'm frustrated by changes to the plans.

4. _____ People would describe me more as a cynic than a Pollyanna.

5. _____ I expect to get what I want when I go after it.

(continued)

(continued)

6. _____ I'd rather work with people who are accommodating and friendly versus tough and competitive.

7. _____ I get defensive when a coworker disagrees with me.

8. _____ It's important to me that my coworkers acknowledge my accomplishments.

9. _____ I tend to see the glass as half empty.

10. _____ It's a challenge for me to be on time.

11. _____ I believe that the needs of the worker are more important than the needs of the company.

12. _____ It's difficult to work on a committee and try to accommodate everybody's ideas.

13. _____ It's important for me to have a boss who compliments me when I'm doing my job well.

14. _____ I have difficulty owning up to my mistakes.

15. _____ I have difficulty saying what I mean in a concise manner.

16. _____ I enjoy being the talker rather than the listener.

17. _____ I don't like to tap-dance around people's feelings; I tell it like it is.

18. _____ I believe in the saying, "If you want it done right, do it yourself."

19. _____ I prefer to put myself first.

20. _____ I am very guarded against negative feedback.

21. _____ I am most comfortable working in a supportive and nurturing environment.

22. _____ I get annoyed when other people achieve more than me or acquire more than me.

23. _____ I have to force myself to attend to details.

24. _____ I get annoyed with coworkers who can't see my point of view.

25. _____ I am impatient when it comes to my career; I deserve more challenge, creativity, and responsibility.

26. _____ I believe that social gatherings and "feel-good" activities are a waste of time.

27. _____ I have trouble identifying my weaknesses when completing performance evaluations.

28. _____ It's important for me to get regular feedback from my coworkers.

29. _____ I prefer projects in which I get to make the final decisions.

30. _____ I deserve a job that is challenging but also allows me plenty of personal time.

31. _____ I prefer a highly flexible work environment over a highly structured one.

32. _____ I believe that I have more skills and abilities than the great majority of my coworkers.

33. _____ It's much more important to be respected than liked.

(continued)

(continued)

34. _____ I have a tendency to take minor criticisms and blow them out of proportion.

35. _____ I value coworkers who address issues and concerns with me in a sensitive and caring way.

Part 2 Scoring

For each PITA type below, add the scores from the survey for the question numbers listed next to each PITA type. Place the total on the line in front of each type. For example, for PITA Type #1: The Sealed PITA, if your scores on question 7 = 4, question 14 = 5, question 20 = 5, question 27 = 5, and question 34 = 4, your total score for the Sealed PITA would be 4 + 5 + 5 + 5 + 4 = 23. High scores indicate that you might have potential for behaving like that type of PITA in certain work situations. Look at your total scores across each PITA to see which are highest. You'll be asked to present your highest three scores on the "My PITA Profile" summary at the end of this chapter.

_____ TOTAL—PITA Type #1: The Sealed PITA
(Add numbers 7, 14, 20, 27, and 34)

_____ TOTAL—PITA Type #2: The Crusty PITA
(Add numbers 4, 9, 17, 26, and 33)

_____ TOTAL—PITA Type #3: The Overstuffed PITA
(Add numbers 2, 8, 16, 22, and 32)

_____ TOTAL—PITA Type #4: The Soggy PITA
(Add numbers 6, 13, 21, 28, and 35)

_____ TOTAL—PITA Type #5: The Sloppy PITA
(Add numbers 1, 10, 15, 23, and 31)

_____ TOTAL—PITA Type #6: The Rigid PITA
(Add numbers 3, 12, 18, 24, and 29)

___ TOTAL—PITA Type #7: The Royal PITA
(Add numbers 5, 11, 19, 25, and 30)

Identifying PITA Situations

Following are two questions for each PITA type, asking you to identify work situations and coworkers that tend to bring out that type of PITA in you. It's important to try to pinpoint where and when your more prominent PITA behaviors tend to show up so that you can strategize how to manage them more effectively.

Which work situations tend to bring out sealed behaviors in you?

_____

_____

_____

Who are the people in your workplace who tend to bring out sealed behaviors in you?

_____

_____

_____

Which work situations tend to bring out crusty behaviors in you?

_____

_____

_____

Who are the people in your workplace who tend to bring out crusty behaviors in you?

(continued)

(continued)

_____

_____

_____

Which work situations tend to bring out overstuffed behaviors in you?

_____

_____

_____

Who are the people in your workplace who tend to bring out overstuffed behaviors in you?

_____

_____

_____

Which work situations tend to bring out soggy behaviors in you?

_____

_____

_____

Who are the people in your workplace who tend to bring out soggy behaviors in you?

_____

_____

_____

Which work situations tend to bring out sloppy behaviors in you?

_____

_____

_____

Who are the people in your workplace who tend to bring out sloppy behaviors in you?

_____

_____

_____

Which work situations tend to bring out rigid behaviors in you?

_____

_____

_____

Who are the people in your workplace who tend to bring out rigid behaviors in you?

_____

_____

_____

Which work situations tend to bring out royal behaviors in you?

_____

_____

_____

(continued)

(continued)

Who are the people in your workplace who tend to bring out royal behaviors in you?

_____

_____

_____

Part 3: Determining the Fit Between Your PITA Behaviors and Your Job

This third area of assessment examines and differentiates your prominent PITA behaviors (identified earlier in part 2) that fit well with your current position from those behaviors that don't fit well. Knowing the fit that exists between your job and the various PITA types and behaviors will help you to prioritize which of your prominent PITA behaviors you need to work on sooner and which ones aren't as urgent to deal with right away.

For example, if you tend to be overly sensitive but work as a pre-school teacher, your sensitivity probably fits better with the pre-school environment and would most likely be perceived more as a strength than a weakness. Therefore, your tendency to be over-ly sensitive might not be an issue in this work environment. If, however, your chosen profession is a trial lawyer, you might need to develop thicker skin (or change careers).

My PITA Profile

Part 3: The Compatibility Between Your PITA Behaviors and Your Job

For each of the seven PITA types, use the following scale to explore how well specific PITA behaviors might be compatible with your current position. *Please note that this scale is different from the one used in the first two parts of the PITA Profile.* You won't enter a number and compute a score.

To be more precise about this process, go to O*NET Online at http://online.onetcenter.org and find the occupation that best matches your current position. You can enter a keyword or browse a Job Family to find the best occupation match. Once you find the occupational title that best fits your current position, click on that title and you'll receive a ton of useful information related to that particular occupation, including tasks (duties), skills and abilities required to do the job, and work styles that fit that job. This additional information should help you rate the degree of compatibility that exists between the different PITA behaviors and your current position. For example, if your job requires a high level of attention to detail, you may rate the compatibility between sloppy behaviors and your current position as "very bad." On the other hand, due to the need for precision and detail, you may view the compatibility between rigid behaviors and your position as "very good." It will be helpful to refer back to the corresponding PITA chapters to remind yourself of the PITA characteristics.

(continued)

(continued)

Very Good

Good

Average

Bad

Very Bad

_____ The compatibility between **Sealed** Behaviors and my current position

_____ The compatibility between **Crusty** Behaviors and my current position

_____ The compatibility between **Over-stuffed** Behaviors and my current position

_____ The compatibility between **Soggy** Behaviors and my current position

_____ The compatibility between **Sloppy** Behaviors and my current position

_____ The compatibility between **Rigid** Behaviors and my current position

_____ The compatibility between **Royal** Behaviors and my current position

Part 4: Assessing and Determining Your Relevant Honorable-Mention PITAs

In chapter 10, we listed 10 other types of PITAs that didn't belong on the main menu but were interesting enough to offer as appetizers on a sampler platter. In other words, these 10 are considered mini-PITAs in that they usually aren't as problematic as the main-menu PITAs, but they can be annoying. So although we're not going to assess their relevance and impact as thoroughly as we did for the main-menu PITAs, we will give you an opportunity to briefly determine which Honorable-Mention PITAs are (a) most annoying for you to work with and (b) most reflective of you and your tendencies.

My PITA Profile

Part 4: Most Significant Honorable-Mention PITAs

Even though we present a brief description of each honorable mention PITA below, it will be helpful to refer back to chapter 10 to refresh your memory about each type of PITA.

The Most Annoying Honorable-Mention PITAs to Work With

Rank from 1 to 10 the most annoying Honorable-Mention PITAs to work with in your opinion, with 1 being the most annoying and 10 being the least annoying.

_____ **Moldy PITA:** Resistant to change—"Why fix it if it ain't broken?"

_____ **Cheesy PITA:** Overuses catch phrases—"synergy, cutting-edge, seamless transition"

_____ **Hot-n-Spicy PITA:** Dramatic and emotional—"It was such an amazing night!"

_____ **Loaded PITA:** Involved in too many things—"I have way too much on my plate!"

_____ **To-Go PITA:** Social butterfly in high gear—"I gotta run [on to the next person]!"

(continued)

(continued)

_____ **Porta-PITA:** Like porta-potties, full of crap—"You look fabulous in that outfit."

_____ **BLT PITA:** Overuses hokey acronyms—"ACE = Accelerate and Cultivate Energy"

_____ **Overcooked PITA:** Belabors points and prefaces everything—"Before I tell you this..."

_____ **Mushroom PITA:** Hoards info and keeps you in the dark—"That's all you need to know"

_____ **Edgy PITA:** Borders on saying things that are inappropriate—"A priest walks into a bar..."

The Honorable-Mention PITAs Most Reflective of Me

Rank from 1 to 10 the Honorable-Mention PITAs that are most reflective of you and your tendencies, with 1 being the most reflective and 10 being the least reflective.

_____ **Moldy PITA:** Resistant to change—"Why fix it if it ain't broken?"

_____ **Cheesy PITA:** Overuses catch phrases—"synergy, cutting-edge, seamless transition"

_____ **Hot-n-Spicy PITA:** Dramatic and emotional—"It was such an amazing night!"

_____ **Loaded PITA:** Involved in too many things—"I have way too much on my plate!"

_____ **To-Go PITA:** Social butterfly in high gear—"I gotta run [on to the next person]!"

_____ **Porta-PITA:** Like porta-potties, full of crap—"You look fabulous in that outfit."

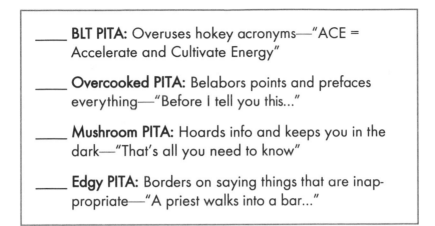

_____ **BLT PITA:** Overuses hokey acronyms—"ACE = Accelerate and Cultivate Energy"

_____ **Overcooked PITA:** Belabors points and prefaces everything—"Before I tell you this..."

_____ **Mushroom PITA:** Hoards info and keeps you in the dark—"That's all you need to know"

_____ **Edgy PITA:** Borders on saying things that are inappropriate—"A priest walks into a bar..."

Computing Your PITA Profile and Establishing Your Action Plan

Using the scores and ratings you completed in each of the four parts of this chapter, complete the "My PITA Profile" template on page 184. This will give you a one-page, personalized snapshot of your most challenging types of PITAs to work with and avoid becoming (to some degree). If your third and fourth ratings are tied, you need to be the judge regarding which one belongs on your PITA Profile. For example, in part 3, if you had two PITA types with a "Very Bad" compatibility rating and two other PITA types with a "Bad" compatibility rating, you'd need to choose between your two Bad-fit PITAs to determine which you believe is the least compatible. Remember that this is not an exact science, but rather something for you to start with and reflect upon.

In chapter 12, you'll learn more about change strategies. You'll refer back to your PITA Profile to develop a concrete, personalized action plan that will enable you to work more effectively with PITA coworkers and decrease your potential to behave like a PITA.

My PITA Profile

Top Three PITA Types Most Challenging to Work With
(Part 1)

_____

_____

_____

Top Three PITA Types I Have Potential to Behave Like
(Part 2)

_____

_____

_____

Top Three PITA Types That Are Least Compatible with My
Current Position (Part 3)

_____

_____

_____

Top Three Most Annoying Honorable-Mention PITAs to
Work With (Part 4)

_____

_____

_____

Top Three Honorable-Mention PITAs Most Reflective of
Me (Part 4)

_____

_____

_____

CHAPTER 12

A Personal Approach to PITA Change

W hen we told a colleague that we were writing a book about PITAs, his response was, "Well, we are all someone's PITA." We laughed because we knew that it was true and that on any given occasion, with the right set of circumstances, anyone can be the PITA. We were also quick to point out that the more important message is that we are all PITAs of the other kind (Professionals Increasing Their Awareness) and that we are on a journey to increase our understanding of ourselves and our relationships with our coworkers, our teams, and our work organizations.

This chapter is intended to help all of us who recognize that we have some PITA tendencies. You will see terms such as "style," "tendencies," or "type" used to describe behaviors because most of us would not consider ourselves full-fledged PITAs; rather, we acknowledge that there are attitudes and behaviors we would like to explore further.

If you have made your way through the preceding chapter, you have at least entertained this thought and might be curious about your own PITA style and how to improve it. Now that you have some sense of your tendencies, we hope you have a couple of questions running through your head, such as, "Okay, so how do I do something about it?" or "Aren't these styles difficult to change because they are linked to personalities?" or "What if I just don't want to change and I'm okay with my style?" These are all legitimate and honest questions that deserve some lively discussion.

We believe that if you have the desire, you can work on, alter, and even change your behaviors, given enough awareness and practice over time. So, having taken a closer look at your style through the activities in chapter 11, let's move on to some preparation and action steps for change. The sections that follow provide you with some other areas to consider, some key questions for you to ask yourself, and some suggestions for helping you through a behavior change.

Taking a Balanced Look at the PITA Types

At different points throughout this book, we have attempted to communicate that PITA behaviors are not *always* bad. We believe that people are by and large good and that they develop behaviors that work for them in some situations and work against them in others. If you're considered a real PITA, however, your proportion of PITA behavior has gotten out of whack and the annoyances and frustrations these behaviors cause seem to overshadow the good.

Okay, so big deal if you exhibit an abundance of Sloppy PITA behaviors, right? I mean, maybe you really enjoy the spontaneous and creative process that comes from living free from the restrictions of following rules, working under timelines, answering e-mail, and turning in reports promptly. You have determined that the priority you place on creativity, the flow of ideas, intuition, and "out-of-the-box" thinking overrules the attention you give to other qualities such as structure, order, exactness, and a focus on the details. So maybe you work in a world where your kind of energy is tolerated and appreciated and not viewed as PITA behavior at all.

If you think in terms of "fit" between personality style and workplace culture, perhaps Sloppy PITA behavior is better accommodated in more unstructured environments. A few work cultures come to mind, such as a creative department of an advertising agency, a university classroom in English literature, a think tank, and perhaps even software design departments. This is not to say that these work cultures don't require a high level of commitment and focus—just not the same level of nonsloppy behavior as, say, a bank, an accounting firm, a chemical laboratory, or an operating room. These latter cultures do not reward a free-spirited approach to work to nearly the same degree.

So evaluating the compatibility of PITA behavior is complex. It requires each of us to think about our behaviors on a number of levels, including our fit with our current job tasks and work roles and our organizational cultures. Other positions and other work environments might be more accommodating to the style we bring to the table.

The Importance of Motivation in Changing Behaviors

We can all attest to the fact that change of any kind is not easy, and ordinarily we do not embrace it. Well, sometimes we embrace it if the change means that we will make more money, have a bigger house, meet someone interesting and exciting, or retire somewhere in the Bahamas. Too often, however, change is forced on us when we would just as soon have kept things the way they were. As with most change, there has to be a moderate to high degree of motivation, which is usually prompted by either gaining something positive as the result of the change, like the beachfront Bahamas condo, or avoiding something negative as the result of the change.

For example, you might have some level of awareness that the crusty behaviors of grumbling and complaining are not very welcome during a planning meeting for the company picnic (as you learned in chapter 3). But your motivation not to grumble and complain might be very low unless there are perceived rewards or punishments associated with the behavior. If it has been your life-long dream to hold the position of "senior events planner" in your company, you probably realize that complaining and grumbling and other crusty behaviors are not going to be your ticket to this coveted position. As a result, you might be highly motivated to change your crusty behaviors. Similarly, if you believe that the planning committee is getting frustrated with your crusty behaviors and that one more grumble about "bad food" or "lame activities" is going to land you off the committee for good, you might also have some motivation for taking a serious look at change.

The point is that the motivation is as necessary an ingredient for change as is the awareness of your own behaviors and tendencies. You can have sufficient awareness, but if the commitment to a change of behaviors is not there, you might still be stuck in patterns that are not working for you. To this end, it is important to honestly assess your level of motivation. Here are some questions you might want to consider to test your level of motivation for change:

1.   Does your style create a level of distress (sadness, frustration, stress) for you?

2.   Does your style cause problems for your coworkers?

3. Do you believe your style negatively affects your performance?

4. Do you believe your style has gotten in the way of a potential promotion(s)?

5. Do you believe that your style has negatively impacted your compensation?

6. Do you care that your performance might have been impacted by your style?

7. Do you care if your style causes problems for your coworkers?

An honest evaluation of these types of questions means really knowing and understanding the things that you care about. Some of us are motivated by personal gain and the rewards and consequences associated with our level of professionalism. Others of us are socially sensitive and team-oriented and we care about the way people in our workplaces respond to us. Whatever your source of motivation, you have to ask yourself whether it's enough to begin engaging in a plan to alter your behavior. If you answered "No" to questions 1–5 in the preceding list, you are probably in good shape, and the strategies that follow can be more about an ounce of prevention than a pound of cure.

Very important: If you answered "No" to all the preceding items, go back one more time and add the word "sometimes" to the end of each question. If you still answered "No" for all the items, you have mastered effective behaviors in the workplace. If a "Yes" has now appeared, congratulations: There's always a little room for improvement.

Preparation for Behavior Change

Now that you have considered the degree of fit between your style and current position and the organizational culture, as well as your level of motivation for change, it's time to put yourself in the right frame of mind for approaching some change strategies. This means adopting a position of openness and acceptance and maintaining a positive outlook as you explore and try out new behaviors. We are believers in the power of positive self-talk and self-statements when trying to tackle new approaches to work and work relationships. Breaking old patterns is not easy. It requires being patient with yourself and realizing that change does not happen overnight.

Here are some messages that you might want to adopt to help you with your plan of action:

1. You are capable of making positive changes in your life.

2. Small changes can produce big results.

3. You have a right to be more content in the workplace.

4. No one is perfect and everyone is a work in progress.

5. Be patient with yourself and tolerant of your setbacks.

6. You can achieve what you set your mind to doing.

7. Be able to laugh at yourself and don't take yourself too seriously.

8. Laugh with others and don't take them too seriously.

9. Your successes will create positive energy for your team and your organization.

10. Become part of a group of "Professionals Increasing Their Awareness."

You might also have your own favorite self-statements that have provided you with motivation, strength, and comfort in the past. Do not hesitate to get out your sticky notes and put these reminders on your mirrors at home, your computer monitors, and your desktops. It takes practice to develop the right mindset to change. So even if many of these statements are hard to believe in the beginning, keep repeating them. Any message that conveys truth, patience, lightheartedness, and understanding has the power to persuade and transform.

The Cognitive Behavioral Approach to Change

By now you're thinking about any PITA styles that you might possess or tendencies and/or patterns that you might want to improve on. We hope that you're also in the right mindset for considering some strategies for behavior change. Now it's time to arm yourself with some tools for carrying out your plan of action.

We draw heavily on the principles from Cognitive-Behaviorism, a theoretical perspective from the field of psychology that is considered one of the more applied, practical, and action-oriented approaches to changing and altering behaviors. There are many forms and nuances to Cognitive-Behaviorism, depending on the theorist whose works you might read and the problems that he or she sets out to tackle. A few of the most notable Cognitive-Behavioral theorists are Dr. Aaron Beck, considered to be the father of cognitive therapy; Dr. Albert Ellis, the developer of an approach called Rational Emotive Behavior Therapy; and Dr.

Donald Meichenbaum, known for a specific Cognitive-Behavioral approach called Self-Instructional Training.

Some core features of Cognitive-Behavioral Therapy, which also make it highly usable in tackling workplace behaviors, are its emphasis on understanding the thoughts that precede or coexist with behaviors, its emphasis on trying out new behaviors in the actual setting where change needs to take place, and its emphasis on changing behavior based on positive and negative consequences. We particularly like the Cognitive-Behavioral techniques because they are straightforward, they can be self-taught and self-administered, and with practice they can produce results in a relatively short amount of time.

The techniques that follow have been adapted from the Cognitive-Behavioral literature (Beck 1995, Ellis 1996, Ellis & Harper 1997, Freeman & Dattilio 1992, Meichenbaum 1974, and Wolpe 1990) based on how they can be applied to workplace behavior and the ease with which you can use them without the help of another person. Although you might have already gotten some useful ideas from each of the individual PITA chapters, the following techniques give you additional tools that you can apply to many examples of behavior change.

Choose the techniques that appeal most to you and those that you believe will be most helpful to you in making the desired changes.

Change Your Thinking: Cognitive

This first group of techniques focuses more on how you think and making changes on the thoughts (cognitions) level. When you are more aware of your thoughts and make changes to your thought processes, behavioral changes can soon follow.

- **Adopt self-statements for better coping:** It is important to be equipped with a repertoire of self-statements as you approach new behaviors. We provided you with a sampling of self-statements in the preceding section, but you can adapt them and even create your own favorites. The beauty of self-statements is that you can carry them anywhere at any time. Because they are part of your internal messaging system, you can make them a regular part of your work life. Other examples of coping self-statements in the workplace could be "I am capable of developing new skills with enough practice" and "I will not let other people's opinions of me keep me from important goals."

- **Dialogue with yourself:** Talking to yourself really doesn't mean you are crazy! In fact, self-dialogue is a way to play out potential conversations in your head, coaching yourself on more-ideal responses and talking yourself out of less-desirable responses. Self-dialogue can be supportive or forceful, depending on your needs at the time. For example, if your "soggy" style is flaring up and you are noticing a high need for affirmation and support from coworkers, maybe some self-dialogue that provides your own "pats on the back" would fit the bill. A useful message might be "I don't need my coworkers' praise right now. While it might feel good, I know that my performance was generally strong and that is enough for me right now."

- **Challenge your "absolute" thinking:** Sometimes people have ways of thinking that are too black-and-white, meaning that they think too much in terms of absolutes. Examples of this type of thinking are beliefs that "I have to be right all time or I will be seen as incompetent" or "I have to perform the best on the team or else I am a loser."

To challenge absolute thinking means that you teach yourself to be okay with being right "some of the time" and that being "a contributing part of a team" can be as valuable as being best on a team. For someone who has overstuffed tendencies, for example, challenging absolute thinking might be a useful antidote to always having to be star of the show.

- **Check your immediate thoughts:** These are the thoughts that go on in our heads, often unnoticed, and are largely unconscious. Almost always, a very quick and immediate thought occurs that precedes our behaviors. If we slow down a bit, we can become more aware of the thoughts. Practicing this level of self-awareness creates the potential for making positive changes. Using the Sealed PITA style, for example, it would be very helpful to know why a person immediately closes herself off when she receives even the mildest feedback on her performance. If she were able to slow down and in a noncritical way look at her immediate thoughts, she might notice that thoughts such as "I must always be right," "This means I am a poor worker," or "People don't like me" are forcing her to close off. The advantage of knowing these thoughts is that she can then challenge them and replace them with more-balanced messages.

- **Develop new insights:** You really can't underestimate the role of insight in changing behaviors. Although many of the cognitive and behavioral interventions are well suited to many types of problem behaviors, insight is often needed to understand issues at a deeper and more fundamental level. Insight has an emotional component that helps you to truly understand why some behaviors might be problematic and how these behavioral patterns are often rooted in early learning experiences. For example, the Combo Sealed, Crusty, Overstuffed PITA like Darryl in chapter 9 might never truly understand why he gets so angry when people leave his organization until he does some soul searching and asks himself some hard questions such as, "Why do I get so agitated and angry when people leave my company?" and "Why do I see other people's successes as my failures?"

Change Your Actions: Behavioral

This second group of techniques is focused more on the actual activity or behavior to be changed. So they tend to fall in the behavioral camp of interventions as opposed to the cognitive. Although these techniques might have a thought component, they emphasize the implementation of the change.

- **Develop a new visual representation:** By imagining yourself in a situation in which you are changing a behavior pattern, you can play out the scenario successfully in your head in preparation for a real-life interaction. For example, if you want to tone down some overstuffed tendencies, practice visualizing a common workplace situation in which you would typically seek out the power and attention. If it's an important meeting with people you would normally want to impress, imagine giving the floor to one of your colleagues and passively sitting back and listening. How does it feel to imagine your colleague getting credit for an idea? How does it feel to get his appreciation for not jumping in?

- **Utilize positive role models:** Use someone in your workplace as a model for the behavior that you are trying to develop or achieve. We believe that many people already do this unconsciously for all types of behaviors they might want to adopt. You can certainly learn from people who seem to have mastered certain behaviors such as effective speaking, organizational skills, or group facilitation ability. For example, if you tend to be sloppy in terms of your abilities to manage detail, stay on task, or stick to deadlines, be sure to notice and study people in your workplace who are very organized. What techniques do they use? How do they plan? How do they prioritize?

- **Play out different roles:** Role-playing is an excellent way to practice behaviors that you would like to be able to adopt as your own. It allows you to rehearse a verbal response or a behavior so that you can try it on before the actual situation takes place. For workplace scenarios, you could use a trusted coworker or friend to assist you with your desired interaction. For example, if you possess a rigid style, you might want to try on some other types of responses to situations in which you ordinarily would need control or power. With your partner, practice being more laid back, more open, and more willing to allow for multiple perspectives.

- **Weigh out the costs and benefits:** By sorting out the costs and benefits of a behavior or action, you can take a logical, reasoned approach to whether it normally produces the best outcomes for you. A cost-benefit analysis can be as elaborate as making written lists that weigh the pros and cons of certain ways of behaving. Or when you need in-the-moment responses, you could learn to do quick cost-benefit analyses in your head. Imagine how useful it could be for the crusty type to take a more thoughtful approach to his responses instead of shooting off abrasive comments from the hip. If he really weighed out the short- and long-term costs of his comments, he might be able to muster some more-balanced responses that don't frustrate and anger his coworkers.

- **Implement rewards and consequences:** Often it's motivating to reward yourself with a treat of some kind for a task that you did well. It can also be just as motivating if you prescribe some sort of consequence if you do not meet your goals. When trying out new behaviors, the same system can help you increase the likelihood that the behaviors that you practice will become habitual over time. If you are a bit high on the Royal PITA scale, make it your goal to practice "other-oriented" or "team-oriented" behaviors. Reward yourself with a cappuccino or some personal leisure time on those days when you have been particularly good at pitching in and thinking beyond yourself. Often the feeling of being a "giver" rather than a "taker" is its own reward.

- **Get training on a new skill:** Often the new behavior that you are seeking really does not come very naturally, and it requires some formal, structured training followed by practice. After all, it's not fair to expect you to go out and try a new way of communicating if you don't know how to do it in the first place. In these cases, maybe a workshop, a seminar, a good self-help book, or counseling/coaching could help you develop the skill. For example, in the case of a soggy style, some instruction on assertive communication skills might be helpful. For someone with the crusty style, some formal work on social skills could make a difference in his way of expressing himself.

- **Be the teacher:** There is the old saying that if you *really* want to learn a topic, you should teach it. There are many opportunities within most work environments to perform professional-development activities that help employees. If you don't want to do it in your workplace, maybe volunteering in the community with adults or high school students might be more to your liking. Pick a topic area that interests you, such as "working effectively on teams," "resolving conflicts," or "conducting efficient meetings," and become knowledgeable in the area.

A Systematic Plan of Action

Now you are equipped with an understanding of your PITA challenges from chapter 11, and you are armed with a series of strategies for working on challenging behaviors from the preceding section. Now you can start to put together a plan of action that will allow you to address problem areas you identified from the "My PITA Profile." As with any plan of action, a systematic approach will keep you focused and on track. The components of your plan could include the items in the following worksheet. It might help you to refer back to your PITA Profile at the end of chapter 11.

1.   The thoughts and behavior(s) that I would like to target for coping more effectively with problematic coworkers in my workplace are

_____

_____

_____

2. The more desirable thoughts and behaviors that I would like to adopt and apply when dealing with problematic coworkers are

    _____

    _____

    _____

3. The thoughts and behavior(s) that I would like to change from my own individual PITA tendencies are

    _____

    _____

4. The more desirable thoughts and behaviors that I would like to adopt and apply when dealing with my own individual PITA tendencies are

    _____

    _____

    _____

5. As I anticipate work environments/scenarios that give me the most problems (identified in chapter 11), I would like to make the following adjustments:

    _____

    _____

    _____

6. As I anticipate interactions with coworkers who present me with the most difficulty (identified in chapter 11), I would like to make these adjustments:

_____

_____

_____

7. The cognitive and behavioral techniques (from the preceding list) that I would like to use to help me with my goals are

_____

_____

_____

8. The people I will ask to support me and check in on my progress are

_____

_____

_____

9. My time frame for noticing some progress in meeting my goals is (be realistic here—behavior change requires patience and takes more than a couple of days)

_____

_____

_____

Documenting Your Progress

It's very important that you create a system for monitoring your progress as you proceed through your days and weeks of trying out new behaviors. This enables you to recall your progress, and it reminds you of your successes. It also informs you whether you need a change of strategy or whether you need to incorporate new techniques into your plan.

We believe that the best way to document your progress is by writing down a small narrative about your interactions. This does not need to take more than a couple of minutes. You could even wait until you get home to jot down some notes. Journaling, as this technique is known, is a valuable tool for developing insights into behaviors. It can also be a great method for coping with stress and emotional discomfort.

Consider this an abbreviated form of journaling. Your note-taking could include the following items:

- What were the specific thoughts and behaviors that you were addressing?

- What did you try differently this time?

- How did you feel when trying on new ways of thinking and behaving?

- What was the outcome?

- Was it satisfactory to you?

- Were there any techniques that were particularly helpful?

- How would you like to do it differently next time?

Research Support and Rationale for *The PITA Principle*

E stablishing positive working relationships has always been an important concept in the world of work. It has, however, historically taken a backseat to intellectual ability, technical competence, and field-specific knowledge when it comes to career success and strong work performance. Employers mostly interpreted team building, open communication, good morale, and developing positive relationships as "soft and fluffy." The term "soft skills" became widely used to describe relationship-building skills and qualities, such as communication, interpersonal skills, teamwork, empathy, tact, and diplomacy.

Over the past 10 to 15 years, an increasing amount of compelling research indicates a heightened importance of soft skills (in other words, relationship-building skills) when realizing career success and top-quality work performance. Because *The PITA Principle*'s primary emphasis is on building and maintaining more positive working relationships, we wanted to share a small yet important sampling of this research. After all, being able to "work with and avoid becoming a pain in the ass" is all about soft skills and building positive working relationships.

Personality and Interpersonal Ability Are the Difference Makers

Increasingly, one's personality and interpersonal strengths are the difference makers when it comes to career success and advancement. From the 2005 *Harvard Business Review* study, "Fool vs. Jerk: Whom Would You Hire?" Casciaro and Sousa Lobo found that, regardless of the type of organization or industry, participating employees preferred working with a friendly and competent coworker over a mean and incompetent one. What was more interesting (and not as obvious) is that people cared considerably more that their coworkers were friendly than competent. They're willing to overlook friendly coworkers' competence deficits, but they're totally unwilling to work alongside a competent jerk.

Another study, commissioned by the TRACOM Group (Leflein Associates, Inc., 2005), surveyed training executives from 100 U.S. companies. Out of the 100 training executives, 94 percent confirmed the importance of interpersonal skills in building and maintaining worker relationships, communicating effectively, managing conflict, and retaining valued employees.

Through their hiring decisions, employers have increasingly demonstrated that they value employees who possess a positive personality and strong interpersonal abilities. The National Association of Colleges and Employers (NACE, 2000–2007) surveys hundreds of employers each year, asking them to rate skills and qualities they seek in graduates. Over the past seven years, interpersonal skills and character traits have dominated the top six:

- Communication

- Honesty and integrity

- Interpersonal skills

- Teamwork

- Motivation/initiative

- Strong work ethic

When asked why softer skills such as interpersonal skills and teamwork are now being rated higher than technical skills, recruiters frequently respond that trying to find a graduate with technical skills is easy these days—they come a dime a dozen. What's tougher to find are graduates who can relate well with coworkers, resolve conflicts tactfully, and communicate their ideas clearly. And it's much harder to teach softer skills, which are deeply embedded into workers' personalities.

Recruiters realize that these softer skills separate the average technically savvy graduate from the high-performing technically savvy graduate. Recruiters want to hire people who are "big" people—people who won't make waves, can handle conflicts tactfully, can work with a wide variety of people, and are unselfish team players. In short, recruiters want to hire people who are not PITAs.

The Shift from IQ to Emotional Intelligence

Thanks in great part to the work of Daniel Goleman and his book *Working with Emotional Intelligence* (1998), employers are much more aware of the major impact that soft skills have on career success. Based on numerous studies that analyze factors influencing job performance, Goleman concludes that emotional competence has a greater impact on job success than IQ does. The seeds of emotional intelligence were planted in the 1970s. Based on his 1973 paper "Testing for Competence Rather than Intelligence," Professor David McClelland of Harvard University concluded that soft skills (for example, empathy and self-discipline) served as better predictors of job success than academic proficiencies did.

It's important to emphasize two underlying concepts of emotional intelligence as it relates to the world of work. The first of these is that emotional intelligence significantly contributes to positive working relationships. This really is the essence of why we wanted to write this book. Our main goal is to help people work together more effectively. That's why we offer strategies to help you cope with difficult coworkers and strategies for keeping your own PITA tendencies in check. The second underlying concept is that emotional intelligence seems to be something that can be learned throughout life. We would not be writing this book if we didn't wholeheartedly believe that people have the ability to change their interpersonal tendencies and behavioral patterns. This book will not only help you to respond more favorably to PITA coworkers, but also to adjust your own PITA tendencies positively.

Leadership Success Requires Interpersonal Effectiveness and Emotional Intelligence

Most professionals in the workplace become leaders in some capacity. Whether you become a CEO or merely mentor a younger coworker, your leadership ability will come into play sometime during your professional career. No matter what leadership role you're in, it's helpful to examine the impact that personality and interpersonal skills have on leaders and how leaders who aren't interpersonally effective can become PITAs.

Caring, Empathetic Leaders Are Most Successful in Today's Workplace

To become a successful leader or executive today, one must possess a positive, caring personality. In a recent article, "Leadership:

Nice Guys Finish First" (Citrin, 2006), it appears that the old authoritarian approach to leadership might not be the most effective way to go. Based on research conducted by the executive search firm Spencer Stuart, 90 percent of the top executives reportedly are unselfish and other-oriented, caring greatly about the success of their subordinates. In summary, those who work constructively with others and are not a pain in the ass are ones who advance in their careers and become effective leaders.

Rigidity and Poor Relationships Are the Most Common Traits Among Ineffective Leaders

In 1996, the Center for Creative Leadership (Leslie and Van Velsor, "A Look at Derailment Today") conducted executive derailment studies to help identify common traits among business executives who failed as leaders. The two most common traits were rigidity (including the lack of openness to feedback) and poor relationships.

Three concepts of *The PITA Principle* relate to the traits found in this study:

- First, negative reaction to feedback is a key concept of the Sealed PITA you read about in chapter 2. Not being able to take an honest look at oneself and own one's weaknesses make it extremely difficult for a PITA to change.

- Second, as mentioned in chapter 1, there is a second type of PITA we're hoping all professionals become: Professionals Increasing Their Awareness. To realize positive change and avoid becoming a pain in the ass, you must increase your sensitivity and openness to feedback about your negative behaviors.

- Third, it's important to point out that one of the seven types of PITAs profiled in this book is the "Make-Your-Own PITA"—also referred to as the "Rigid PITA."

There is also an obvious connection between PITAs and the second most common trait among failed leaders, poor relationships. Pain-in-the-ass employees usually have poor relationships with their coworkers because nobody really enjoys being around a PITA.

The Difference Between Successful Managers and PITA Managers

The derailment study conducted by the Center for Creative Leadership (Leslie and Van Velsor) also revealed characteristics of successful managers that included conscientiousness, trustworthiness, and strong social skills. These characteristics of emotional competence are consistent with what we believe makes up a healthy, productive professional. Many of the types of PITAs that we describe in the book do not possess these types of characteristics.

The Heightened Importance of Building Relationships

We hope that you're already convinced that building positive work relationships with your coworkers (even the PITAs) is paramount to career success and work performance. But just to put the icing on the cake, consider a few potential opposing forces to building positive relationships and avoiding becoming a PITA: the evolution of technology, a value shift in mass media, and helicopter parenting.

The Evolution of Technology and Its Impact on Face-to-Face Interaction

There are so many positive outcomes from the pervasive evolution of technology: increased communication with a wider array of people, enhanced efficiency of work flow and distribution, and e-commerce, to name just a few. But as in all of life, there needs to be a healthy balance. Typically, when there is a significant change in lifestyle, you get something new but have to give up something in the process. One of the major concerns with the emergence of our high-tech world is the impact it has on face-to-face interaction and communication.

Employers Are Concerned About Graduates' Communication Skills

There appears to be a growing concern among employers regarding the interpersonal and communication ability found in graduates and young employees today, contributing to a further widening of the communication gap. In a 2005 article in the *Pittsburgh Post-Gazette* (online)—"Employers Complain About Communication Skills"—reporter Jim McKay expressed a growing sentiment among employers of college students, that whereas college students are undeniably tech-savvy, they lack verbal communication skills.

In the same article, Debra Vargulish, a recruiter for Kennametal, Inc., observed that college students are somewhat shy and have trouble with the most elementary communication, including handshakes and introductions.

The Internet, Technology, and Social Isolation

The Internet has had a profound impact on the way we do business and communicate with each other. As previously mentioned, this unique tool offers a plethora of assets. However, based on a study conducted at the Stanford Institute for the Quantitative Study of Society (Dixon, 2005), there is strong evidence that the Internet is negatively impacting social interactions. Based on the study, those who use the Internet more frequently spend 70 minutes less daily interacting with family.

It's not only the Internet that is keeping our youth from interacting with people. Today, kids and teens have so many different types of screens and things to interact with—TV, computer, video games, MP3 players, cell phones—making it tough for old-fashioned, face-to-face activities and interaction to compete. For each of life's tasks, healthy development depends on ample time spent experiencing or practicing that particular life task. Just as a skier won't develop into an effective skier without ample practice, an employee won't develop into an effective face-to-face communicator without enough time spent communicating in person with others.

When conflicts occur, there is no substitute for sitting down face-to-face with your coworker and working things out. It's important to not only listen to what your coworker is saying, but also to observe and pick up on his or her nonverbal cues. Seeing the anxiety in your coworker's eyes and noticing his or her facial expressions of concern are huge when you're trying to assess the level of conflict with which you're dealing. Young people today are trying to resolve conflicts via texting, e-mailing, and phone conversations more than ever. Looking somebody in the eye and addressing a serious issue is not something they've experienced as frequently as previous generations have. Such a disconnect contributes to the growing isolation that many people feel and stands in the way of resolving conflicts.

The Value Shift in Mass Media

It's difficult to measure the effect that changing values in the mass media have on working relationships, but common sense would tell us that the major values shift that has occurred over the past 30 to 40 years must have some degree of impact. Our professional opinion is that the most significant shift in values within the mass media can be characterized as one of disrespect for people. Just take a look at the evolution of three forms of mass media: video games, television, and music.

The Evolution of Video Games

More and more preteens and teenagers are playing video games these days, and the most popular games seem to be the most violent and offensive. For example, one of the most popular video games today is Grand Theft Auto (GTA), in which players earn points by killing police officers and beating up prostitutes.

The goal of video game manufacturers is to make it as true to life as possible. They want you to feel like you're actually there, experiencing the "game" firsthand. Take a look at what appeared on the Grand Theft Auto Web site as it was trying to lure our youth into buying its third version of GTA:

> *GTA3 will be much more than just a pretty face, and as usual if you're not interested in the missions there will be laws to break, people to beat up, grannies to mug, and vehicles by the hundreds to carjack. The living, breathing city theme remains, and as in GTA2 you are just as likely to get carjacked or beaten up as any of your hapless victims are. Thanks to the third dimension though, the game will be a lot more in your face than the previous two, where you sometimes felt quite isolated from your little head and shoulders on the ground below. (www.rockstargames.com/ grandtheftauto3/)*

Wow, isn't it just great that kids and teens will feel much more as though they are beating up grannies and carjacking vehicles!

The Evolution of Television

Whatever happened to the days when saying "stinker" on TV was a big no-no? Do you remember the episode of *The Brady Bunch* when Greg and Marcia called Bobby a stinker, and Mrs. Brady scolded them for using such an offensive word? Over the years, it's hard not to notice the gradual decline of respect for parents and family members in general. From *My Three Sons*, to *Leave it to Beaver*, to *Little House on the Prairie*, to *The Brady Bunch*, to *Family Ties*, to *Married...With Children*, to *The Simpsons,* there has been a gradual shift from total respect for parents to almost total disrespect. This has at least some degree of impact on how people think about and treat their supervisors and bosses, let alone their coworkers.

The Evolution of Music

The main cover story and special report by Nancy Gibbs on *Time* magazine's July 31, 2005, edition was entitled, "Being 13." The report highlighted an evolution of music, contrasting the #1 song on the *Billboard* charts in 1953 with the #1 song on the charts in 2005. The article points out that in 1953, Percy Faith and His Orchestra's "Song from Moulin Rouge" contained tender and innocent lyrics related to being in love. In stark contrast, the 2005 top song from 50 Cent, "Candy Shop," presented lyrics that were sexually graphic and tasteless.

This values shift in the mass media (video games, TV, music) is characterized by a gradual yet profound decline of respect for others and for humanity in general. Although there aren't studies that directly correlate this values shift with working relationships, there are plenty of studies indicating that people become desensitized with increased exposure. For example, the more that people become exposed to songs and TV shows depicting a lack of respect for others, the more they become desensitized to disrespectful behavior—behavior characterized by many PITAs, especially Crusty, Royal, and Overstuffed.

Helicopter Parenting

"Helicopter parenting" is the term used to describe the overly involved and protective parenting style of many baby boomers. As with the mass-media shift in values, it's difficult to measure the impact that helicopter parenting may have on children's future ability to build strong relationships at work. However, with conflict resolution being such an important dynamic in maintaining strong work relationships, there is growing concern that helicopter parents—who hover over their kids and swoop them up out of harm's way—are not giving their children enough space to experience adversity firsthand and learn how to cope with difficult people. They are also possibly creating the next generation of PITAs (see chapter 8, "The Royal PITA") by giving them such a sense of entitlement.

In 2004, Hara Estroff Marano wrote a thought-provoking article in *Psychology Today* called "A Nation of Wimps," pointing out the hyper-concern that today's parents have for their children and the impact it might have on their ability to handle adversity and conflict. In it he pointed out that by sheltering children from all types of hurt and danger, parents have actually made them more fragile. Today, kids, teens, and even young adults are in constant contact with their parents, thanks mostly to cell phones. The "Nation of Wimps" article addressed this concern as well, claiming that this constant communication with mom and dad is stifling our children's independence and ability to work out conflicts on their own.

Summarizing the Research Implications Related to *The PITA Principle*

In summary, there is growing evidence that suggests the increased importance of building positive relationships in the workplace, especially in today's world. The ability to interact effectively with all types of coworkers is instrumental in getting a job, advancing in one's career, and performing work at a high level. This is easier said than done, especially when you're working with some difficult personalities. Anybody can build positive relationships with friendly and accommodating coworkers. *The PITA Principle* is designed to help you enhance relationships with difficult coworkers and to improve on your own interpersonal behaviors in order to begin shaving off layers of PITA tendencies that exist inside you.

References

Beck, A. T., & Freeman, A. T. (1990) *Cognitive therapy of personality disorders.* New York: The Guilford Press.

Beck, J. S. (1995). *Cognitive therapy: basics and beyond.* New York: The Guilford Press.

Casciaro, T., and Lobo, M. S. "Competent jerks, lovable fools, and the formation of social networks." *Harvard Business Review.* Vol. 83, No. 6, June 2005.

Citrin, J. M. (2006). "Leadership: Nice guys finish first. Leadership by example." Retrieved February 8, 2006, from http://finance.yahoo.com/expert/article/leadership/2513.

Dixon, K. (2005). *Researchers link use of Internet, social isolation.* Stanford Institute for the Quantitative Study of Society.

Ellis, A. (1996). *Better, deeper, enduring brief therapy: The rational emotive behavior therapy approach.* New York: Brunner/Mazel.

Ellis, A., & Harper, R. A. (1997). *A new guide to rational living* (3rd ed.). North Hollywood: Wilshire Books.

Freeman, A., & Dattilio, F. M. (1992). *Comprehensive casebook of cognitive therapy.* New York: Plenum.

Gibbs, N. (2005, August 8). "Being 13: A special report." *Time. 166*(6), 40–63.

Goleman, D. (1998). *Working with emotional intelligence.* New York: Bantam Books.

Grand Theft Auto Web site, www.rockstargames.com/grandtheftauto3/.

Leflein Associates, Inc. (2005). *A research study on Interpersonal Effectiveness Training (IET).* The TRACOM Group.

Leslie, J. B., & Van Velsor, E. (1996). *A look at derailment today: North America and Europe.* Center for Creative Leadership, Greensboro, NC.

Marano, H. E. (2004, Nov.–Dec.). "A nation of wimps." *Psychology Today.* Vol. 37, Iss. 6, 58.

McClelland, D. C. (1973). "Testing for competence rather than intelligence." *The American Psychologist, 28*(1), 1–14.

McKay, J. (2005, February 6). "Employers complain about communication skills." *Business News, Post-gazette.com.*

Meichenbaum, D. (1974). "Self-instructional training: A comprehensive prosthesis for the aged." *Human Development, 17,* 273–280

National Association of Colleges and Employers. (2000–2007). *Job outlook surveys.* Bethlehem, PA.

Ogilvie, J. R., & Carsky, M. L. (2002). "Building emotional intelligence in negotiations." *International Journal of Conflict Management, 13*(4), 381 (20 pgs.).

Peck, M. S. (1978). *The road less traveled*. New York: Simon & Schuster, Inc.

Peck, M. S. (1983). *People of the lie*. New York: Simon & Schuster, Inc.

Peck, M. S. (1994). *A world waiting to be born: Civility rediscovered*. New York: Bantam Books.

Rode, R. C., Mooney, C. H., Arthaud-Day, M. L., Near, J. P., Baldwin, T. T., Rubin, R. S., & Bommer, W. H. (2007). "Emotional intelligence and individual performance: Evidence of direct and moderated effects." *Journal of Organizational Behavior, 28*, 399–421.

Shipper, F., & Dillard, J. E. (2000). "A study of impending derailment and recovery among middle managers across career stages." *Human Resource Management Journal, 39*, 331–345.

Shipper, F., Kincaid, J., Rotondo, D. M., & Hoffman, R. C. (2003). "A cross-cultural exploratory study of the linkage between emotional intelligence and managerial effectiveness." *International Journal of Organizational Analysis, 11*(3), 171 (21 pgs.).

Thomas, A., & Chess, S. (1977). *Temperament and development*. New York: Bruner/Mazel.

Wolpe, J. (1990). *The practice of behavior therapy* (4th ed.). New York: Pergamon.

Yukl, G., & Falbe, C. M. (1990). "Influence tactics and objectives in upward, downward, and lateral influence attempts." *Journal of Applied Psychology, 75,* 132–140.

Index

A PITA Seminar for Your Organization

If you like what you've read in *The PITA Principle* and think your organization would benefit from participating in a PITA seminar, Dr. Robert Orndorff and Dr. Dulin Clark are available for on-site training tailored to the specific needs of your organization.

PITAs at Work: How to Deal with and Avoid Becoming a Pain in the Ass

Seminar Overview

Surveys by the National Association of Colleges and Employers indicate that the "softer skills" of interpersonal effectiveness and character assets are ranked of highest importance among business recruiters. Business can literally be won and lost based on the interpersonal effectiveness and character of your employees.

In this seminar, the authors of *The PITA Principle* and JAZ consultants Drs. Orndorff and Clark focus heavily on the concept of self-awareness as a core ingredient to better interpersonal effectiveness with clients, customers, and coworkers. Only through an honest self-assessment of strengths and growth areas can there be a starting point for improvement. Orndorff and Clark highlight seven types of PITAs found most prevalently in the workplace (plus various "combos"). This seminar offers strategies for working more effectively with each type of PITA and becoming more aware of your own tendencies toward being difficult to work with in certain work situations.

Seminar Takeaways

- Develop an understanding of the patterns associated with difficult personalities through a humorous look at the PITA. Develop an understanding that nobody is exempt from being a PITA now and then.

- Build up self-awareness around your strengths and deficits in the areas of interpersonal effectiveness and communications. Become part of a group of "Professionals Increasing Their Awareness."

- Develop strategies for becoming more confident and effective during difficult interpersonal situations. Participants will practice responding to PITAs as they present themselves in the workplace.

- Learn additional interventions that can be used in many work situations and contexts.

Half-day and full-day training programs are available based on the needs of your organization.

Contact JAZ Consulting to schedule a PITA Seminar:

bob@jazconsulting.org
www.jazconsulting.org

Visit the PITA Blog

To expand on the conversation about workplace effectiveness and self-awareness, we're blogging at *The PITA Principle* **blog:**

http://pitaprinciple.blogspot.com

Join us there as we

- **Introduce additional PITA types:** This is your chance to be creative in introducing completely new and different PITA types and descriptions not already included in *The PITA Principle*.

- **Share readers' coping strategies:** Although we've offered many strategies for working with difficult people, other people no doubt have additional ideas. We want to hear about any strategies you have found to be effective when working with specific personality types.

- **Share self-improvement success stories:** It's just as important to identify your own PITA behaviors and how you manage them. If you have been successful in curbing your PITA tendencies, how have you done so? We'd love to hear.

- **Participate in the general discussion:** We'll talk about the importance of self-awareness (an accurate understanding of your strengths, weaknesses, and motivations) to having constructive workplace relationships.

E-mail us at **pitaprinciple@yahoo.com** with your suggested new PITA types, coping strategies, success stories, and general discussion topics.